Clinical Child Psychology Library

Series Editors: Michael C. Roberts and Annette M. La Greca

ANXIETY AND PHOBIC DISORDERS
A Pragmatic Approach
Wendy K. Silverman and William M. Kurtines

AUTISM
Understanding the Disorder
Gary B. Mesibov, Lynn W. Adams, and Laura G. Klinger

INFANT AND EARLY CHILDHOOD NEUROPSYCHOLOGY
Glen P. Aylward

MANAGING MANAGED CARE
Michael C. Roberts and Linda K. Hurley

PARENT–CHILD INTERACTION THERAPY
Toni L. Hembree-Kigin and Cheryl Bodiford McNeil

SEXUALITY
A Developmental Approach to Problems
Betty N. Gordon and Carolyn S. Schroeder

A Continuation Order Plan is available for this series. A continuation order will bring delivery of each new volume immediately upon publication. Volumes are billed only upon actual shipment. For further information please contact the publisher.

Autism
Understanding the Disorder

Autism
Understanding the Disorder

Gary B. Mesibov and
Lynn W. Adams
University of North Carolina
Chapel Hill, North Carolina

and

Laura G. Klinger
University of Alabama
Tuscaloosa, Alabama

Plenum Press • **New York and London**

Library of Congress Cataloging-in-Publication Data

Mesibov, Gary B.
    Autism : understanding the disorder / Gary B. Mesibov and Lynn W.
Adams and Laura G. Klinger.
        p.   cm. -- (Clinical child psychology library)
    Includes bibliographical references and index.
    ISBN 0-306-45546-3 (hardbound). -- ISBN 0-306-45547-1 (pbk.)
    1. Autism in children--Psychological aspects.   I. Adams, Lynn W.
II. Klinger, Laura G.   III. Title.   IV. Series.
    [DNLM: 1. Autism.   WM 203.5 M578a 1997]
RJ506.A9M48   1997
618.92'8982--dc21
DNLM/DLC
for Library of Congress   97-35645
                                                                 CIP

ISBN 0-306-45546-3 (Hardbound)
ISBN 0-306-45547-1 (Paperback)

© 1997 Plenum Press, New York
A Division of Plenum Publishing Corporation
233 Spring Street, New York, N. Y. 10013

http://www.plenum.com

10 9 8 7 6 5 4 3 2 1

Preface

This volume is designed to provide a comprehensive overview of autism for the many educated and thoughtful parents, professionals, and other concerned citizens with an interest in these important issues. It has grown out of our assumption that there are many people interested in our field who want the most up-to-date information available without having to locate and read through the growing literature in this area. From our university bases, we are fortunate in having access to state-of-the-art information about autism and related developmental disorders. Our goal in this volume is to synthesize this information and present it comprehensively and objectively.

This volume is the culmination of 2 years of hard work identifying, organizing, writing, rewriting, and editing the most up-to-date information available about people with autism, their families, and the state-of-the-art about the nature, causes, underlying mechanisms, diagnosis, and treatment of autism. We hope it will help the many friends, colleagues, families, and interested citizens who have expressed their interest in a publication of this kind.

Acknowledgments

A project of this scope could not have been completed without the help of many fine friends and colleagues, too numerous to name. As with all of our professional activities we are indebted to our TEACCH colleagues and the many families and professionals we know in North Carolina, around the United States, and throughout the world for their interest, support, insights, and generosity in sharing their ideas and observations. We hope that our final product reflects their many superb contributions.

Many TEACCH staff and University of North Carolina students contributed substantially to this endeavor. In our TEACCH office Jill Cagle was as competent, cheerful, and industrious in helping with our secretarial and administrative needs as she is with the many TEACCH projects she undertakes. J.P. Barfield's support and assistance is also appreciated. In addition to administrative and secretarial help and support, J.P. carefully and meticulously typed the many drafts of this manuscript that our collective compulsiveness generated. Leigh Cantrell, an undergraduate research assistant, is among the most pleasant and accurate students we have ever encountered during our careers. Leigh carefully read and reread many drafts for typographical and related editorial clarity. If there ever was a mistake that she missed during the months that she worked with us we are certainly unaware of it.

Thanks also go to Michael Roberts and Annette LaGreca, the series editors. Michael and Annette took their responsibilities very seriously, reading our first draft carefully and contributing many invaluable suggestions. To the extent that this manuscript is clear and reader friendly we have Michael and Annette to thank.

Finally, Mariclaire Cloutier from Plenum is the perfect editor. She is always positive, helpful, and supportive. At the same time, Mariclaire is never afraid to call and remind us when the next draft should be moving along more quickly. Her blend of support and encouragement are the reason why this project was completed in a timely fashion.

Of course our families and friends deserve a debt of gratitude for enduring our ill tempers and time away from home that a project of this scope involves. We hope that they will enjoy the final product and feel it is worthy of their many sacrifices.

Contents

Prologue 1

1. Historical Background 3

Introduction 3
Original Kanner Description 4
Psychoanalytic Theory 6
  Arguments against Psychoanalytic Theory 8
Early Biological Formulations 10
  Seizures 10
  Electroencephalogram Studies 10
  Nystagmus 11
  Prenatal and Perinatal Insults 11
  Hyperoxia 11
  Congenital Rubella 12
  Physical Anomalies 12
Genetic Theories 13
Suggested Locations of Neurological Dysfunction 14
  Neurochemical Theories 14
  Hemispheric Lateralization 14
  Reticular Formation 15
Early Behavioral Formulations 15
Summary 17

2. Definition of the Syndrome 19

Current Diagnostic Criteria 21
  Reciprocal Social Interaction 21
  Verbal and Nonverbal Communication 22
  Restricted Repertoire of Activities and Interests 24
  Signal Detection 24

Early Diagnostic Markers 25
Associated Characteristics 25
Diagnostic Tools 26
    Childhood Autism Rating Scale 26
    Autism Diagnostic Observation Schedule 27
    Prelinguistic Autism Diagnostic Observation Scale 27
    Parent Interview for Autism 27
    Autism Diagnostic Interview 28
History of the Definition of Autism 28
    Autism as a Pervasive Developmental Disorder 31
Epidemiological Data 32
    Prevalence 32
    Are Cases of Autism on the Rise? 32
    Prevalence in Siblings 33
    Sex Ratios 33
    Mental Retardation 34
    Social Class Distribution 34
Differential Diagnosis 35
    Autism and Other Pervasive Developmental Disorders ... 35
    Autism and Mental Retardation 37
    Autism and Learning Disabilities 38
    Autism and Attention Deficit Disorder 39
    Autism and Obsessive-Compulsive Disorder 40
    Autism and Developmental Language Disorders 41
    Autism and Schizophrenia 42
Summary 43

3. Current Biological Theories of Causation 45

Genetic Findings 45
    Is Autism a Severe Form of a Genetic Disorder Causing
        Social and Cognitive Impairments? 46
    Is Autism Caused by Several Different Genetic
        Abnormalities? 47
    Summary 50
Prenatal and Perinatal Complications 50
Neuroanatomical Findings 51
    Cerebellum 52
    Limbic System 53
    Cerebral Cortex 54

Brain Size 55
Summary 55
Cortical Electroencephalographic Findings 56
Patterns of Brain Activity 56
Seizure Disorders 58
Landau–Kleffner Syndrome 59
Summary 60
Neurochemical Findings 60
Serotonin 60
Brain Opioids 61
Summary 62
Conclusions 62

4. Language and Cognition **65**

Language Abilities 65
Semantic Aspects of Language 66
Pragmatic Aspects of Language 67
Emotional Perception and Expression 68
Memory 69
Attention 71
Theory of Mind 73
Executive Functions 74
Summary 75

5. Intervention Approaches **77**

Psychodynamic 77
Biological Interventions 78
Anticonvulsant Medications 79
Neuroleptics 79
Stimulants 80
Tricyclic Antidepressants 80
Beta-Blockers 81
Lithium 81
Fenfluramine 81
Naltrexone 81
Megavitamin Therapy 81
Summary 82
Educational/Behavioral Interventions 82

Operant Approaches 82
Cognitive Behavioral Approaches 84
Social Learning Approaches 86
Summary 91

6. Controversial Treatment Issues 93

Early Intervention 94
Normalization 97
Inclusion 98
Supported Employment 99
Punishment 101
Labeling and Specialization 102
Facilitated Communication 103
Summary 104

Epilogue 105

References 107

Index 119

Prologue

Autism was first described in the literature by Leo Kanner in 1943. Kanner was fascinated and intrigued by the social withdrawal, communication peculiarities, insistence on sameness, and other idiosyncracies of the 11 children he identified as different from the children whom he typically housed in his Child Inpatient Unit. Parents and professionals who have studied autism following Kanner have also been captivated by these children. The enormous range of behaviors, unique patterns of strengths and weaknesses, inconsistencies in performances, communication and social impairments, and preoccupations, among other things, have led to much speculation about autism and the fundamental problems these youngsters face.

This volume will begin with Kanner's description and trace what we have learned about autism in the past 50 years. Although autism is a relatively new area of inquiry, much has been determined about possible causes; treatment mechanisms; the ways people with autism think, learn, and understand; family dynamics; and strategies for integrating people with autism into our communities. Each of these will be examined in turn with an emphasis on the information that will be most applicable to those working with these clients in community-based settings.

As we learn more about people with autism, we realize how difficult it can be for them to function effectively in our schools and society given the nature of their social, communication, conceptual, sensory, and behavioral problems. On the other hand, we are encouraged and inspired by what they can achieve when they work with parents and professionals who understand their strengths and possibilities. This volume will not only offer perspectives describing what we know about the deficits related to autism but will also present teaching strategies that have proven effective and accomplishments that have exceeded our expectations.

Historical Background

Peter had always been a difficult baby. He cried frequently, and although his mother tried to comfort him, he was inconsolable. He never reached for his mother to pick him up. When she did hold him he did not cling to her. But, since he was her first child, his mother took her friends' and relatives' advice not to worry. She hoped that Peter would eventually grow out of it. When Peter joined a play group of toddlers his age, the differences between him and other children became impossible to ignore. He did not appear to notice the other children. He always played alone. Every day, in the midst of a noisy room of rambunctious children, Peter moved around quietly collecting all of the stuffed animals into a pile. Peter's parents suspected that he was deaf and asked their pediatrician for a referral to a specialist.

Lauren was the youngest of six children, and the only daughter in her family. Her brothers were happy to include her in their play, and fought over who would care for her. She loved to be held and sung to. Her early development was similar to that of her brothers. She babbled at the age of six months, and began using single words shortly after her first birthday. By the age of 18 months, Lauren was using about 25 words, mainly to request food and favorite toys. Lauren stopped speaking several months before her second birthday. Relatives suggested that she had so many people to care for her that she did not need to speak. However, also at this time she developed some odd behaviors. She began to sit in her crib rocking back and forth when she woke up, whereas she had formerly cried to be picked up in the morning. Also, she became fascinated by objects she could spin and ignored her other toys. She refused all food except for pureed squash. When her pediatrician found no physical problems, she referred Lauren to a child development center.

Joey's mother was pleased that he had always been totally different from his older brother, Michael. Whereas Michael was very active, into everything, and boisterous, Joey was a quiet baby who rarely cried. Joey's mother was relieved that he would sit calmly in her lap while she kept an eye on the troublemaking Michael. It became a family joke that Joey was just like his father, a university professor. Joey was also a very happy baby who enjoyed being bounced on his father's knee, listening to music, and playing with pots and pans. He could entertain himself in this way for very long periods of time. When he was 9 months old, Joey began humming to himself in his crib. His parents were amazed at his ability to carry a tune, and as he grew older he demonstrated a remarkable memory for tunes he had heard just a few times. Although Joey's family celebrated his unique personality and talents, they began to worry when at the age of 18 months he had not begun talking. His parents suspected that he was mentally retarded, but could not reconcile this suspicion with his talent for music and his normal motor development. Perplexed, they decided to have him evaluated for a developmental disability.

Although these three children began life with strikingly different temperaments and family circumstances, by the age of 2 they will all meet criteria for the same diagnosis: autistic disorder. How did these children, who share the social, communication, and behavioral symptoms of autism but came to the attention of professionals in such different ways, develop the disorder? This question has perplexed parents and professionals since Leo Kanner first gave autism a name in 1943. This chapter will chronicle the efforts of professionals whose insightful theories—and whose unfortunate but necessary mistakes—have laid the groundwork for our current understanding of autism.

ORIGINAL KANNER DESCRIPTION

In his 1943 paper "Autistic Disturbances of Affective Contact," Leo Kanner described the syndrome that he called early infantile autism. He presented thorough and insightful case descriptions of 11 children who, although similar to each other, were strikingly different from the children with whom they had often been associated, those diagnosed with childhood schizophrenia. Kanner's genuine interest in the children he described was immediately evident from the first sentence of his landmark paper: "Since 1938, there have come to our attention a number of children whose condition differs so markedly and uniquely from anything reported so far, that each case merits—and, I hope, will eventually receive—a detailed consideration of its fascinating peculiarities" (Kanner, 1943, p. 217).

Although Kanner viewed infantile autism as distinct from childhood schizophrenia, he concluded that when children with autism grew up they were likely to develop schizophrenia (Eisenberg & Kanner, 1956). Three observations led him to conceptualize autism as a distinct disorder:

1	Even those children with autism who developed normally for the first 18–20 months of life began showing signs of the disorder well before any child diagnosed with schizophrenia showed signs of psychosis
2	Follow-up studies of children diagnosed with autism revealed that none of them developed hallucinations, a common feature of schizophrenia
3	There was far less history of psychosis in families of children with autism than in families of children with schizophrenia (Eisenberg & Kanner, 1956)

Kanner's perceived link between schizophrenia and autism was social isolation. In fact, he used the term *autism*, defined as immersed within oneself, because he viewed social withdrawal as the primary feature of this new disability he defined (Kanner, 1949). He emphasized that the social isolation was different from the withdrawal from preexisting social relationships seen in schizophrenia. Rather, Kanner stated that, "There is from the start an *extreme autistic aloneness* that, whenever possible, disregards, ignores, shuts out anything that comes to the child from the outside" (Kanner, 1943, p. 242). He noted that children with autism did not show a preparatory response to being picked up, were content to play alone, and treated people as objects. Another defining feature was insistence on sameness. He observed that the children strictly followed many routines, becoming very upset at any changes in their rituals. Kanner also described language impairments and deduced that these resulted from the children's social isolation. Their language was characterized by echolalia, extreme literalness, and pronominal reversal (e.g., referring to self as "you" and others as "I").

Kanner's three areas of emphasis—social isolation, insistence on sameness, and abnormal language—continue to be the three primary features of autism. Kanner's paper provided a clear and detailed account of the disorder's defining features and is still a valuable resource for those who wish to better understand autism. Nevertheless, because of the relatively few cases of autism that Kanner encountered during his career and the lack of other studies or papers, some of his beliefs about the disorder have proven inaccurate as information about children with autism has accumulated.

One such belief was that most children with autism exhibit average or above-average intelligence. Kanner believed that the children he observed had normal intellectual potential, based on peak skills in such areas as rote memory and musical ability. Kanner also thought that the parents of these children were strikingly intelligent and came from higher social classes than did parents of his patients who did not have autism. As will be discussed in the next chapter, these findings were later demonstrated to reflect referral biases and do not represent actual trends.

Another belief that has since been widely refuted was that the etiology of autism was at least partly psychogenically based. Although Kanner originally believed that autism was present from birth, his studies revealed no unusual childhood illnesses or neurological abnormalities, probably because of small sample sizes and the lack of today's diagnostic sophistication. Thus, Kanner was unable to formulate any biological hypotheses about the etiology of autism. This led him to examine his clients' family functioning. He described a "mechanization of human relationships," obsessiveness, and lack of parental warmth (Kanner, 1949, p. 421). He hypothesized that children with autism reacted to inadequate parenting by seeking comfort in solitude. It is now known that any behavior that differentiated these parents from those of children who did not have autism was a result, rather than a cause, of autism in their child. Indeed, Kanner was not completely satisfied with this psychogenic formulation for two reasons: (1) many of the children he observed had siblings who did not have autism, and (2) other parents with the same characteristics did not have children with autism. Although Kanner himself remained skeptical of his psychodynamic theory, much of the autism research that followed was psychodynamically oriented.

PSYCHOANALYTIC THEORY

In attempting to explain the strange behaviors of children with autism in psychodynamic terms, early theorists focused on the difficulty the children had with relating to others, especially their parents. If children with autism could not relate to others, their repetitive actions, language impairments, and other symptoms must, these theorists reasoned, represent a withdrawal from an outside world that they found intolerable. Ruttenberg hypothesized that autism was "a disorder of emotional development" that affected the formation of object relationships, disturbing the child's progression through psychosexual stages (Ruttenberg, 1971, p. 148). Children with autism, then, were fixated or regressed at an early stage of development; therefore, treatment should logically involve reactivation of "the stalled developmental process" (Ruttenberg, 1971, p. 148). Like many other psychodynamic theorists, Ruttenberg suggested nurturant mothering contact from childcare workers as the treatment of choice. With this successful object relationship, the children would be able to differentiate themselves from others, reactivating their arrested psychosexual and ego development. Mahler (1952) believed that children with autism did not differentiate their mothers from inanimate objects; thus, they could not establish emotional ties with them. This led to a withdrawal from both internal and external stimuli, a shutting-out of the outside world and its demands for affective responses.

If children with autism withdrew from object relationships, did they withdraw because of unsatisfactory responses to their attempts at relating, or did they withdraw because of some innate incapability? In keeping with the constant nature–nurture controversy in their field during the 1950s and 1960s, many psychoanalytic theorists believed that the etiology of autism lay on a continuum between biological and environmental factors. They hypothesized that many children had a nonspecific, innate vulnerability that, in the absence of certain environmental mediators, would result in autism.

These theorists proposed that the chief environmental mediator was warm, responsive parenting. Many reports supporting Kanner's hypotheses that parents of children with autism were often cold, obsessive, and unresponsive appeared in the literature (Bettelheim, 1967; Despert, 1951). In these reports, however, questions arose as to whether the behavior noted in the parents caused or resulted from their child's autism. Even Bettelheim, the psychoanalytic theorist who most consistently blamed parents, pointed out that it is hard to separate cause from effect in a relationship as intimate as that between a mother and child. This is especially true when parents are seen by professionals only after they have been living with their child for several years. Ruttenberg (1971) believed that adequate mothering could compensate for the vulnerability. He described an innate vulnerability that interacted with poor parenting to produce autism. This vulnerability, caused by some congenital abnormality or birth trauma, resulted in an impairment in the child's response to mothering.

Bettelheim was skeptical of the biological theories. In his seminal book *The Empty Fortress* (1967), he reasoned that any biological abnormalities present in children with autism were effects, rather than causes, of the disorder. For example, he suggested that an absence of early emotional stimulation damaged the central nervous system (CNS), affecting both ego development and intellectual functioning. Bettelheim's hypothesis that autism was a reaction to emotional deprivation had roots in his studies of concentration camp victims. Having experienced concentration camps firsthand, Bettelheim saw similarities between autistic symptoms and the hopeless withdrawal he observed, and may himself have felt, as a prisoner in a concentration camp. The impact of this horrible experience may have also caused Bettelheim to overemphasize the effects that cold and authoritarian relationships could have on behavior in situations far removed from the concentration camps.

Bettelheim refuted biological theory by asserting that he had cured children of autism using psychotherapy. If the cure was psychodynamic, Bettelheim believed, then the etiology was necessarily psychodynamic also. Because he assumed that parents caused autism in their children, Bettelheim believed that the only way to treat autism was to remove the children from their parents: "Just because it is so extraordinarily important for the infant's well-being and later healthy development to have a good mother, it is erroneously assumed that any mother–child relationship is so valuable that it must be salvaged, even when it is damaging to the child" (Bettelheim, 1967, p. 408). Bettelheim's aim was to nurture the children with positive relationship experiences so that they would feel safe enough to abandon their "autistic defenses."

The task of raising children with special needs and of searching, often in vain, for services for them was difficult enough for parents who had not been told that their coldness caused their children's behavior. Deprived of the chance to raise their children and blamed for their difficulties, many parents suffered needless anguish as a result of the dominance of psychoanalytic theory during the 1950s and 1960s.

Arguments against Psychoanalytic Theory

In the years following Bettelheim's book, theoretical reasoning and empirical research diminished the credibility of the psychogenic arguments. Papers refuting these damaging theories enabled researchers to explore more fruitful etiological possibilities. The early psychogenic theories were called into question by basic epidemiological data: There were more cases of autism in boys than in girls, there were very few families in which more than one child had autism, and very few children with autism had a history of deprivation (Rutter & Bartak, 1971). Questions of whether psychodynamic factors could influence the development of secondary handicaps, or whether they could interact with biological vulnerabilities to produce autism, were not so easily dismissed. Many of the studies supporting psychoanalytic formulations were anecdotal and contaminated by lack of control groups, poor quantification of variables, and clinical observation rather than empirical measurement. Rutter (1967) could not find sufficient evidence for a psychogenic etiology based on these studies and stressed that any difference in the personalities of parents of children with autism was probably a result, rather than a cause, of their child's autism.

The main premise of psychoanalytic theory was the assumption that social withdrawal was the central feature of autism and resulted in the additional impairments in language and repetitive activities. This assumption was discredited by both empirical and clinical observations (Rutter, Bartak, & Newman, 1971). Social difficulties could not account for other impairments, considering that improvement in social functioning did not result in improved intellectual or language capabilities. Also, social impairment could not explain many of the language abnormalities present in autism; rather, it seemed that language problems could just as easily account for social difficulties.

Rutter (1978b) provided a convincing rebuttal of other common notions in psychodynamic theory when he stressed that demonstration of effectiveness in a treatment technique does not necessarily substantiate its underlying theoretical basis. Contrary to Bettelheim's assertion, Rutter claimed effective psychotherapeutic methods did not prove that autism was psychogenically caused. Rutter also stressed that, although psychoanalysts reported successful treatment methods, they had never subjected them to systematic evaluations. Uncontrolled, nonsystematic clinical observations were insufficient evidence for the efficacy of psychotherapeutic methods. Furthermore, Rutter pointed out that the failures in bonding reported by psychodynamic theorists were also readily observed in children raised in institutional settings, but produced opposite results. These children, in sharp contrast to children with autism, became clingy and overly friendly. Also, they typically had normal language development and functioned intellectually within the average range. Children from deprived environments who did have difficulties demonstrated *delayed* rather than deviant language, and improvements in their environments resulted in reversals of their intellectual and language impairments.

The final blow to psychoanalytic theory was the empirical proof that parents of children with autism were no different from parents of children with other types of learning and developmental problems. Cantwell, Baker, and Rutter (1979), using data from interviews, behavioral observations, and personality measures, demonstrated that parents of children with autism and parents of children with dysphasia were no different in intensity and frequency of positive interactions, quality of family interactions, and types and degree of mother–child interactions. Mothers were no different on personality traits such as neuroticism and extroversion. Another study found no differences on the Minnesota Multiphasic Personality Inventory (MMPI) between parents of disturbed children without autism and parents of children with autism (McAdoo & DeMyer, 1978). The same study found that MMPI profiles of parents of children with autism were significantly less pathological than those of adult psychiatric outpatients.

These findings conclusively put an end to blaming parents for their children's difficulties, opening the way for a partnership between parents and professionals that has led to less destructive and more effective treatment approaches for children with autism and their families.

EARLY BIOLOGICAL FORMULATIONS

The fall of psychodynamic theories came, in part, from accumulating evidence on the biological nature of autism. As the evidence against the psychogenic formulations mounted, more attention was focused on neurological and biological aspects and causes of autism. As a result, more attention was focused on seizures, nystagmus, pre- and perinatal insults, and genetic theories. The interest in neurological and biological aspects of autism remains strong today. This chapter reviews some of the earliest theories regarding underlying biological abnormalities in autism. More recent theories are discussed in Chapter 3.

Seizures

The appearance of seizures in many children with autism was one of the first reasons that researchers began to search for biological etiologies. Schain and Yannet (1960) found a 42% incidence of seizures in their sample of children with autism, but that number was later revised to 25–33% (Deykin & McMahon, 1979a; Rutter, Greenfeld, & Lockyer, 1967). This figure, 25–33%, is much higher than the incidence of seizures in the general population. Although seizures usually appear well after the onset of autism, they present clear evidence of brain abnormalities. Because of the different ages of onset, Rutter and Lockyer (1967) suggested that seizures do not cause autism, but rather both disorders result from the same underlying brain pathology.

Electroencephalogram Studies

Reports of seizures in people with autism resulted in increased administration of electroencephalograms, or EEGs. Early EEG investigations found that abnormal EEGs were more common in autism than in the general population. Although researchers agreed on the finding, they disagreed about the nature, cause, and result of these abnormalities. Like seizures, abnormal EEGs suggested neurological dysfunction, a finding useful in further refuting the remaining psychodynamic claims. It was still necessary, however, to determine the specific pattern of the brain's dysfunction in order to derive more information about etiology and treatment, and this effort to identify specific patterns of brain dysfunctions continues today.

Nystagmus

Another observation that interested neurobiological theorists was that some children with autism disliked being swung around and turned upside-down, while others seemed to seek out these disturbances of equilibrium (Ornitz, 1978). It appears that children with autism either fear these sensations or are fascinated by them. Significantly, many children with autism do not seem to become dizzy or lose their balance after long periods of whirling. This absence of nystagmus, the sensations that follow disturbances of equilibrium, suggests a dysfunction in the vestibular system, which is regulated in the brain stem. A dysfunction in this area could explain such phenomena as self-stimulatory rocking and spinning, fascination with spinning objects, delayed motor development, and toe-walking (Colbert, Koegler, & Markham, 1959; Ornitz, 1978).

Prenatal and Perinatal Insults

Studies of birth trauma and complications during pregnancy have yielded useful hypotheses about factors contributing to the etiology of autism. Labor complications, forceps deliveries, abnormal conditions of infants at delivery, and neonatal complications have been shown to be common in children with autism (Lobascher, Kingerlee, & Gubbay, 1970). Lobascher et al. also noted that 13 of their 20 subjects with autism were postmature. They suggested that the risk of intrauterine anoxia increases with postmaturity and may contribute to autism. Taft and Goldfarb (1964) studied pre- and perinatal complications in subjects with autism, their siblings, and developmentally normal controls. These complications were 69% more common in boys with autism than in their siblings, and 56% more common in girls with autism. The researchers noted that, in the general population, more boys than girls sustain brain damage as a result of birth complications. They suggested that the high ratio of boys to girls with autism could indicate the importance of brain damage as a causal factor. Because not all children with autism have histories of birth complications, Taft and Goldfarb hypothesized that several causal factors must combine to produce autism, with pre- and perinatal complications being just a few of the many factors. More recent research on pre- and perinatal complications contradicts some of these early theories and is discussed in Chapter 3.

Hyperoxia

In his seminal book, Rimland (1964) suggested that a congenital defect in the brain stem's reticular formation, an area of the brain responsible for regulating oxygen to the rest of the brain, left children vulnerable to autism. Perinatal complications were seen as one of the environmental stressors that could make this vulnerability evolve into autism. Rimland did not believe that oxygen deprivation, called anoxia, was a cause of autism because: (1) some children with autism had been given oxygen although they were not anoxic, (2) studies had not shown a link between anoxia and autism, and (3) anoxia did not produce the same pattern of brain damage that Rimland expected in autism. Instead, Rimland hypothesized that overoxygenation or hyperoxia might be related to autism. Overoxygenation resulted in a condition called retrolental fibroplasia, which often caused blindness. Rimland suggested that retrolental fibroplasia, not overoxygenation, interacted with a genetic vulnerability to cause autism.

Congenital Rubella

Because of the high incidence of mental retardation in autism and the effects of encephalopathy on intellectual functioning, Deykin and MacMahon (1979b) studied the association of autism with certain viruses. Focusing on the viruses reported to cause encephalopathy if sustained in infancy or during gestation (e.g. measles, mumps, rubella, and chicken pox), Deykin and MacMahon found that children with autism had been exposed to these viruses, and especially rubella, more often than their nonhandicapped siblings. They noted, however, that the exposure rate was still quite low. At the same time Deykin and MacMahon were conducting their work, researchers studying groups of children who had contracted congenital rubella as a result of the 1964 rubella epidemic noted that a subset of their subjects had autism. Based on these findings, Chess (1971) estimated the prevalence of autism in children with congenital rubella at 741 per 10,000, compared to estimates of 3 or 4 per 10,000 in the general population. This was compelling evidence for an association between the two disorders.

Chess (1977) believed that, contrary to some reports, autism was not a result of sensory deprivation due to the blindness and deafness that often resulted from congenital rubella. Based on these observations she suggested that the course of autism in children with congenital rubella resembled that of a chronic infection. The course was characterized by recovery, chronicity, improvement, worsening, and even delayed effects. Because not all children with autism had been exposed to the rubella virus before they were born, Chess concluded that she had identified a subset of children whose autism had a viral cause. She hypothesized that "autism may be the final behavioral consequence of many different causes" (Chess, 1977, p. 81). Perhaps there are several different conditions, and even combinations of conditions, that act on the brain to produce the same disorder.

Physical Anomalies

Despite Kanner's (1943, p. 247) observations that children with autism were attractive and had "intelligent physiognomies," Walker (1977b) noted that their physical appearance was often characterized by minor physical anomalies. The most common anomaly was low-seated ears, but Walker also observed high palates, abnormal head circumferences, abberent earlobes, and gaps between the first and second toes in many subjects with autism. A 1978 study also found more physical anomalies in children with autism than in their siblings or normal controls (Campbell, Geller, Small, Petti, & Ferris, 1978). These researchers noted that anomalies were more often localized in the mouth and ears. To explain how these anomalies might relate to autism, Walker speculated that they suggested a "deviant intrauterine experience" (Walker, 1977b, p. 174); it was likely that they resulted from a problem in development occurring very early in the gestation period. The same early developmental insult that caused the anomaly was hypothesized to have caused the autism.

To broaden his hypothesis, Walker (1977a) studied another expression of very early developmental insult: the patterns of children's fingerprints. Comparing autism to disorders such as Down's syndrome and Turner's syndrome, which result from congenital chromosomal malformations, Walker found that children with autism had more arches and whorls on their fingers than did developmentally normal children and that their finger patterns were also different from those in schizophrenia or mental retardation. This study offered further evidence that autism is a disorder distinct from schizophrenia and mental retardation and that it results from a congenital defect that expresses itself well before birth.

GENETIC THEORIES

The possibility that autism could be genetically determined seemed unlikely to early biological theorists, because no parent of a child with autism had the disorder and it was uncommon for one family to have more than one child with autism. As clinicians became more familiar with the disorder, diagnostic procedures improved, and family histories were examined more closely, it became apparent that autism sometimes did, in fact, affect families more than once.

Working in the late 1970s, Folstein and Rutter (1977) used the purest method of exploring the possible genetic basis of autism: the twin study. Their finding that 4 of 11 monozygotic pairs, as opposed to 0 of 10 dizygotic pairs, were concordant for autism suggested that there was a genetic component. Because there were cases in which monozygotic, or identical, twins were discordant for autism, however, it was clear that autism was not purely genetically inherited. Folstein and Rutter theorized that what is genetically inherited is not autism, but rather some linguistic or cognitive impairment of which autism is one manifestation. Indeed, five of the seven children without autism who were part of a monozygotic twin pair had cognitive, social, or communicative abnormalities. The question became, and remains, what is the factor(s) that causes an abnormality to be expressed as autism? Genetic research is an exciting area of inquiry and will be discussed in depth in Chapter 3.

SUGGESTED LOCATIONS OF NEUROLOGICAL DYSFUNCTION

Neurochemical Theories

Studies of neurotransmitters suggested that the neurotransmitter system may function differently in people with autism. Neurotransmitters are the means by which nerve cells communicate with one another. They are chemicals that are released, as a result of a triggering stimulus, from a neuron to the space between neurons, the synapse. The arrival of the chemical in the synapse stimulates or inhibits the next neuron and changes the likelihood that the cell will fire (Ritvo, Rabin, Yuwiler, Freeman, & Geller, 1978). Ritvo and his colleagues postulate a link between neurochemical regulatory factors within the CNS and neurophysiologic abnormalities (Ritvo, Yuwiler, Geller, Ornitz, Saeger, & Plotkin, 1970). Researchers have studied one neurotransmitter in particular: serotonin. Serotonin regulates sleep, body temperature, and sensory perception and has been implicated in the etiology of seizure and movement disorders and mental retardation. It has also been suggested that serotonin influences the modulation of affect. Many of the functions regulated by serotonin are abnormal in autism (Cohen, Caparulo, Shaywitz, & Bowers, 1977).

Hemispheric Lateralization

Colby and Parkison (1977) found that whereas only 12% of the developmentally normal children in their sample were non-right-handed, this occurred in 65% of their children with autism. They wondered if something related to autism might be causing these children to fail to lateralize normally. Colby and Parkison speculated that left hemisphere damage was probably not the cause because the right hemisphere would compensate for this damage early. Instead, they thought that the damage was bilateral, affecting both hemispheres. Later that same year Boucher (1977) failed to replicate these findings. She did, however, find a small trend in the same direction and a relation between the degree of mental retardation and the length of the delay in establishing normal patterns of hand preference. Boucher's study also demonstrated that the distribution of hand preferences in subjects with autism was similar to that of control subjects matched on verbal ability. She suggested that hand preference was associated with linguistic ability rather than overall ability. Boucher also examined the hand preference of the parents of her subjects and found that more parents of children with autism were right-handed than left-handed. Her findings, she asserted, disconfirmed the hypothesis that there was a genetic link for autism associated with cerebral dominance. More recent research, however, has again raised the question of whether impairments in hemispheric lateralization are characteristic of persons with autism.

Reticular Formation

In his 1964 book, Rimland skillfully called into question the predominant psychogenic theories of the time. In their place, he suggested that researchers concentrate on detecting and examining biological dysfunctions. In particular, Rimland used his book to put forth "a hypothesized relation between the cognitive dysfunction in autism and the reticular formation of the brain stem" (Rimland, 1964, p. 87). Rimland believed that the central cognitive dysfunction in autism was an inability to connect new stimuli to remembered experience. This could cause difficulties in understanding relationships and abstractions and in integrating individual sensations into a comprehensible single concept. For example, he believed that the child with autism does not associate pleasure with his mother because of an inability to link past pleasurable experiences with his mother to a current experience with her.

This dysfunction would, on the other hand, result in facility for rote memory, puzzles, and form boards. Children with autism showed strengths in these areas, Rimland suggested, because they do not require conceptualization. Rimland called these skills and such behaviors as echolalia and pronoun reversal "closed-loop phenomena." Children with autism were able to perceive stimuli, but they stored them in the same form in which they had perceived them, and gave them back without processing them. Rimland wrote, ". . . stimuli are apprehended, but not comprehended" (Rimland, 1964, p. 86).

Although Rimland conceded that his theory was insufficient to account for all of the symptoms in autism, he hypothesized that integration of past experiences with new information took place in the reticular formation in the brain stem and that there may be a lesion or defect in this area. He suggested that the reticular formation was important for both perceptual and conceptual phenomena. As with the genetic work, studies on the possible location of neurological dysfunction have proliferated in recent years. Those studies will be reviewed in Chapter 3.

EARLY BEHAVIORAL FORMULATIONS

In the early 1960s, there was little information about the etiology and treatment of autism. Psychoanalytic theories were still in existence when Ferster (1961) made an important connection between learning theory and autism. In his theoretical paper, Ferster suggested that the behavior of children with autism was maintained by reinforcement and could be controlled through behavior modification techniques. He stressed that the consequences of the child's action were responsible for its frequency. For example, a child who receives a cookie every time he verbally requests one will use verbal requests to fulfill his needs. A child who asks for but does not receive the cookie, however, may resort to other methods, such as tantrums, to have his needs met. If the parent succumbs to the tantrum and gives the child a cookie, the child learns that in order to get a cookie, he must throw a tantrum.

Ferster suggested that the key to extinguishing inappropriate behaviors is discontinuing an undesirable behavior's consequences. In the tantrum/cookie scenario mentioned here, if the child no longer receives a cookie after the tantrum he will learn that tantrums no longer produce cookies. Ferster demonstrated that the same successful behavioral methods used in the laboratory were successful in the day-to-day world of the child who has autism (Ferster & DeMyer, 1961).

Ferster's clearly presented and well-documented formulations led to much valuable research corroborating the effectiveness of behavioral methods in the treatment of autism. Ferster's suggestion that inattentive or depressed parents contributed to the etiology of the disorder by failing to reinforce behavior, however, proved unfounded. As a result of Ferster's positive contribution, Lovaas and his colleagues began a series of experiments that used various behavioral methods to change the behavior of children with autism. A major focus of Lovaas' work was in the area of self-injurious behavior. One method he used to attempt to control these disturbing behaviors was positive reinforcement of other appropriate behaviors (Lovaas, Freitag, Gold, & Kassorla, 1965). Lovaas et al. demonstrated that when reinforced for appropriate behavior a child with autism was more likely to perform that behavior and less likely to perform self-destructive behaviors. The accepted treatment for self-injury at that time had been expressing sympathy for the child by using comments such as, "I don't think you are bad." Psychoanalytic theorists believed that children were self-destructive because they viewed themselves as unlovable. Lovaas et al. demonstrated that sympathetic comments actually represented *positive reinforcement* for self-mutilation and served to increase the behavior. They theorized that the attention a child received for self-destructiveness was a pleasant consequence that led to continued self-injurious behavior.

Lovaas was committed to stopping self-injury and was determined to avoid the common practice of restraining children who would severely harm themselves if left unsupervised. He believed that while positive reinforcement of appropriate behavior was effective, it took too long to extinguish the behavior. While the child was learning more appropriate behaviors, she continued to harm herself, albeit less often than before. Lovaas could not tolerate any self-injury and began to use punishment as part of the treatment plan for self-injury. In a 1974 interview, Lovaas explained that, although it was painful for him, he had concluded that spanking and electric shock were the most practical solutions for self-injurious behavior (Chance, 1974).

Many facets of Lovaas's contribution to the field of autism have been invaluable. Although he strongly adhered to Ferster's application of learning theory, he rejected the notion that parents were at all involved in the etiology of the disorder. At a time when many professionals blamed parents for their children's difficulties, Lovaas empowered parents by involving them in their children's treatment. Lovaas taught behavioral methods to parents and saw them as crucial members of the child's treatment team. Furthermore, Lovaas advocated the rejection of academic theories that lacked empirical support. His treatment methods were developed in the laboratory and tested in the child's real world (Lovaas, Schreibman, & Koegel, 1974). Lovaas's use of empiricism encouraged other professionals to rely on treatment methods that were based on data, rather than on untested theories derived from unfounded ideas about etiology.

Despite these important contributions, many of Lovaas's ideas remain controversial. Although his use of punishment for self-injury may be justifiable as an emergency measure, his use of punishment in teaching speech to children with autism is less acceptable (Lovaas, Berberich, Perloff, & Schaeffer, 1966). Another of Lovaas's beliefs has also caused controversy. In a 1974 interview he stated: "One way to look at the job of helping autistic kids is to see it as a matter of constructing a person. You have the raw materials, but you have to build the person" (Chance, 1974, p. 76). Not only does this suggest that the person with autism is other than—or less than—a person, but it also implies that the professional's job is to change the person.

Lovaas expressed an idea later in the interview that seems more feasible, yet contradicts his theory of "build[ing] a person." Lovaas went on to say that we cannot expect blind children to exist in the same way as sighted children, so we cannot expect children who have autism to exist in the same way as those who do not. As with blind children, it is necessary to change the environment to compensate for the difficulties of the child with autism. Perhaps these two ideas do not need to contradict each other. It is possible to help the child with autism to change, while we also accept the responsibility of changing the environment to better suit that child.

SUMMARY

Following Kanner's original description in 1943, there have been many different views and approaches to problems of children with autism and their families.

Initially viewed as an emotional problem, autism was dominated by psychoana-lytic therapists in the early years, with group therapy for the parents and play therapy for the children. The psychoanalysts also advocated separating children with autism from their families, who were seen as the cause of this severe disability of development.

The 1960s began the end of the control of psychodynamically oriented approaches to autism. Arguing for biological causes, investigators began accu-mulating evidence to support their views. Refuting psychoanalytic theory be-came the focus of research during this decade.

One line of research demonstrated that parents were not the cause of autism; rather, they were a group of parents indistinguishable from any other parents except for having a child with autism. Studies focused on their family interactions, personal characteristics, and general functioning. Research also highlighted their other children, who, in most cases, did not have autism and were normally functioning, effective, and productive individuals. Biological observations and theories also became important. Studies of seizures, EEGs, nystagmus, pre-and perinatal insults, hyperoxia, congenital rubella, and physical anomalies were designed to explore biological differences in these children and to suggest theoretical implications. Theories about genetic differences and neurological dsyfunctions began as a rebuttal to the psychoanalytic claims and continue today. As the evidence mounted against psychoanalytic approaches to autism, the need for alternative treatment approaches became paramount. Be-havior therapy evolved to fill the void with some early impressive demonstra-tions on how children with autism could be successfully taught. These early behavioral interventions have become the cornerstone of several current treat-ment efforts.

Definition of the Syndrome

Mario is a second grader who loves school. He knows how to read, enjoys math, and looks forward every day to art class. He creates pictures that are covered with thick layers of paint and stickers. These cover his refrigerator at home. His teacher has trouble getting him to stop his schoolwork and go outside for recess. Once outside, he prefers to play alone instead of joining the other children's games. His classmates admire him for his artwork and his sticker collection, but wonder why he has difficulty taking turns and sharing. Sometimes Mario has trouble switching activities in class and can be very slow or tearful when starting a new project. He still hasn't found a best friend.

Ned has had many jobs throughout his adult life, but until he got his job in the library he never stayed in a job for more than 6 months. His slowness, poor organization, and aberrant behavior proved difficult for his employers to tolerate. Ned's job performance on a crew that cleaned bathrooms in college dormitories typifies his previous work history. Ned would begin cleaning a bathroom by meticulously scrubbing the sink, using copious amounts of cleaning fluid to combat old stains. This done, he would do a similarly thorough job of cleaning the toilet and mopping the floor. Lastly, Ned rinsed the toilet brush and dumped the dirty mop water into the clean sink. When his employer pointed out the mistake in the order of his cleaning activities, Ned became upset and threw his cleaning supplies against the wall. In his new job at the library, he is often praised for his accurate and independent shelving of library books. Ned takes great pride in his work. The library staff readily accepts his meticulousness and methodical work style, and sensitive coworkers are able to redirect or criticize Ned's performance without upsetting him.

Keisha is a 5-year-old girl who attends a developmental day care center while her parents are at work. She does not speak. When she wants a particular food or toy, she either grabs it herself or takes the hand of her teacher and puts it on what she wants. She is not yet toilet trained. Keisha's main activities are staring at her fingers while she moves them in front of her eyes and rocking back and forth. When upset, she throws herself onto the floor and repeatedly bangs her head. When she is dressed in anything other than cotton clothing, she undresses herself within minutes. Other than this, though, she makes no effort to either dress or undress herself. Her favorite activities are watching her mother vacuum the rugs and riding in the car.

Malcolm is a 19-year-old accounting major at a community college. He makes straight As, and is a member of the chess club. Outside of school, he has no contact with his peers. He lives with his parents, and spends most of his time at home in his room studying military history and listening to Beatles records. He wears the same outfit every day. Malcolm has worked for the past two summers and part-time during the school year at a small accounting firm. The firm is extremely impressed with his work and intends to hire him when he graduates. Malcolm feels confident about his future and happy with his life. His one wish is to find someone to marry. He reads singles magazines hoping to learn how to meet someone compatible.

Although many parents dislike having their children referred to as "autistic," "learning disabled," or "mentally retarded," they are still relieved that there is a physiological reason for their children's behavior and reassured that there is an accepted diagnosis for the condition. Negative reactions to diagnostic labels are understandable. Unfortunately, many parents and professionals believe that diagnosing a child, and thereby identifying that child as a member of a larger group, results in a loss of that child's identity. The fear is that if teachers or other professionals know that a child has autism they may make rigid assumptions about that child based on their knowledge of autism, not on the child's unique personality traits. In this way, characteristics that make a child an individual could be overlooked. This issue will be discussed in greater detail in Chapter 6.

CURRENT DIAGNOSTIC CRITERIA

Since Leo Kanner initially described autism in 1943, the impairments in autism have been grouped into three areas of functioning termed the "triad of impairment" by Wing and Gould (1979):

1	reciprocal social interaction
2	verbal and nonverbal communication
3	a restricted repertoire of activities and interests

DSM-IV divides the diagnostic criteria among these three impairments, requiring that a child meet at least two criteria from the social category and at least one from both the communication and restricted repertoire of activities categories (see Table 2.1).

Reciprocal Social Interaction

DSM-IV lists four criteria for areas of social interaction that are qualitatively impaired or totally absent in children with autism. The first criterion is "marked impairment in the use of multiple nonverbal behaviors such as eye-to-eye gaze, facial expression, body postures, and gestures to regulate social interaction." In the area of eye to eye gaze, a person with autism may avoid eye contact or,

Table 2.1. Comparison of Original and Current Criteria for Autism

Kanner's criteria	DSM-IV criteria
Social isolation	Social impairment
No preparatory response to being picked up	Impaired use of nonverbal behavior
Content to play alone	Lack of peer relationships
Treat people as objects	Failure to spontaneously share enjoyment, interests, and achievements with others
	Lack of reciprocity
Abnormal language	Communication impairment
Echolalia	Lack or delay of language
Extreme literalness	Difficulty initiating or sustaining conversations
Pronominal reversal	Stereotyped, repetitive, or idiosyncratic use of language
	Impairment in pretend play
Insistence on sameness	Restricted repertoire of activities and interests
Follow routines and rituals	Interests which are narrow in intensity or focus
Resistance to change	Routines or rituals
	Motor mannerisms
	Preoccupation with parts of objects

conversely, may stare so intently into the eyes of his listeners as to make them uncomfortable.

With regard to facial expression, a person with autism may display a flat, blunted affect or alternatively may show an inappropriate amount or intensity of laughter or distress. Body postures or gestures may lack nonverbal enhancements such as head nodding, pointing, or the shrugging of shoulders.

The second criterion is "failure to develop peer relationships appropriate to one's developmental level." This criterion can be appropriately applied to children with autism who are uninterested in having friends or who seem to want friends but don't understand how to go about establishing friendships. Some children with autism naively believe that all members of their class are their friends. Others are depressed by their inability to establish friendships. Even the most intellectually advanced person with autism has difficulty articulating what it means to be someone's friend. It is important to note that this criterion emphasizes the appropriateness of friendships relative to developmental level. Thus, a severely retarded person with a mental age of a 2–3-year-old who simply participates in parallel play with others is exhibiting friendship skills at an appropriate developmental level. Inversely, a 10-year-old with intact intellectual skills who is unable to name a best friend is not at an appropriate developmental level.

The third criterion is "a lack of spontaneous seeking to share enjoyment, interests, or achievements with other people." For instance, a child with autism, delighted to see his favorite neighborhood dog on a walk with his mother, may not point it out to her. This inability to share a focus of attention through gesture is different from the ability to use gesture to make a request. The ability to show objects of interest to others typically develops during the first year of life and its absence is one of the earliest symptoms of autism (Baron-Cohen et al., 1996; Osterling & Dawson, 1994).

"Lack of social or emotional reciprocity" is the fourth criterion. For example, a person with autism may monopolize a conversation without realizing that his partner is bored or in a hurry and without soliciting the other person's input on the topic. Conversely, a person with autism may prematurely end a social interaction. For example, a child who is laughing and clearly enjoying having his mother blow bubbles may simply walk away. This would not necessarily mean the child is not attached to his mother. Instead the child might simply have trouble maintaining social interactions, even pleasurable ones.

Verbal and Nonverbal Communication

There are four criteria under the category of impairment in communication as well. The first criterion is "delay in, or total lack of, the development of spoken language" that is not compensated by the use of gesture or other forms of communication. DSM-IV defines delay in language development as a failure to develop single words by 2 years of age and short phrases by 3 years of age. So, a child who doesn't say his first word until 18 months would technically not meet this criterion even though children usually develop first words prior to this time. In determining when language development occurs, it is important to distinguish between babbling (e.g., "mama mama") and the use of a sound to indicate a particular object or person (e.g., "mama" to refer to a mother). Children with autism often exhibit normal babbling but fail to develop the ability to use words to refer to objects/people. Additionally, approximately 37% of children with autism reportedly begin to use first words on time and then suddenly stop talking between 24 and 30 months (Kurita, 1985). If language is not absent, as is the case in half of the people with autism, it is almost always deviant. Examples of deviant language include pronoun reversals (e.g., "you" instead of "I") or echolalia (repeating words or phrases).

The second criterion, "in individuals with adequate speech," is "marked impairment in the ability to initiate or sustain a conversation with others." People with autism often have difficulty choosing a topic for conversation in which the other person is interested. For example, a teenager with autism may avoid talking to females because of an inability to think of anything to say or may always begin conversations by asking his partner's birth date. Also, a person with autism may have an extensive vocabulary that they use to deliver a monologue about a preferred topic but be unable to engage in simple conversations that do not involve this preferred topic.

The third criterion is "stereotyped and repetitive use of language or idiosyncratic language." For example, Kanner (1943) described a child who followed a strict routine before going to sleep, requiring his mother to participate in a scripted conversation that was identical from day to day. Unusual aspects of language including immediate echolalia (repeating a word or phrase immediately after another person), delayed echolalia (repeating entire scripts from television or previously heard conversations), pronoun reversal (referring to the self as "you" and others as "I"), and metaphoric speech (using a phrase as a metaphor, such as saying, "Give me a hand Jack" to mean "I need help") are included under this criterion.

The fourth criterion is "lack of varied, spontaneous make-believe play or social imitative play appropriate to developmental level." Whereas some children with autism may never engage in pretend play, others may insist on playing house according to the same plot, using the same words, with the same people, every time. It is important to examine a child's play with their developmental level in mind. A child with a mental age of 18 months would be expected to exhibit simple pretend play such as holding a telephone up to his ear or feeding a doll, and a child with a mental age of 4 should engage in elaborate thematic play such as pretending that dolls are having a party or setting up an elaborate army battle. Social imitative play involves imitating another person's actions such as their mother's cooking with pots and pans. Children with autism have particular difficulty imitating another person's motor movements (Dawson & Adams, 1984), even though their verbal imitative abilities can be quite good.

Restricted Repertoire of Activities and Interests

The third impairment in the triad, "restricted, repetitive and stereotyped patterns of behavior, activities and interests," involves observably deviant, rather than absent, behavior. The first criterion is "encompassing preoccupation with one or more stereotyped and restricted patterns of interest that is abnormal either in intensity or focus." People with autism may learn vast amounts of information about a highly restricted topic, such as meteorology or geography, often pursuing these interests in a restricted manner by memorizing facts and conversing mainly on their chosen topics. In their play, children with autism may focus on one particular toy (e.g. Legos) or only play with an unusual object (e.g., straws, strings, sticks).

The second criterion is "apparently inflexible adherence to specific, non-functional routines or rituals." Examples of this criterion are demanding to perform a bedtime ritual in a precise order and only eating particular foods served in a particular way (e.g., only eating a sandwich if it is bologna with cheese and mayonnaise and refusing to eat if any of the ingredients is absent or not the expected brand). Additionally, parents often report that even young children with autism are uncommonly aware of driving routes and become upset if a different road is taken.

The third criterion is "stereotyped and repetitive motor mannerisms." Stereotyped body movements such as rocking, hand-flapping, spinning, or head-banging are common, especially among younger and lower-functioning children.

The fourth criterion is "persistent preoccupation with parts of objects." Children with autism may persistently smell their toys, play with toy trucks only by repetitively spinning their wheels, or be obsessed with looking at parts of objects such as door hinges or table tops.

Signal Detection

Along with establishing clear and reliable diagnostic criteria, studies leading up to DSM-IV were designed to determine the relative importance of each diagnostic characteristic. Signal detection studies separate diagnostic from descriptive criteria, identifying key criteria in order to aid clinicians in determining how to weigh the different pieces of information they collect from their clients. These studies determine the predictability of a diagnosis of autism from individual criteria. Siegel, Vukicevic, and Spitzer (1990) determined that the only DSM-III-R criterion with enough predictive power to be a mandatory criterion is "marked lack of awareness of the existence or feelings of others." Other criteria that were sometimes predictive of an autism diagnosis were impaired imitation and absent social play. The criteria of impaired nonverbal communication and abnormal speech were also useful.

Early Diagnostic Markers

Several recent studies have examined early diagnostic markers of autism that are present within the first 18 months of life. These studies have been conducted through retrospective reviews of videotapes (Osterling & Dawson, 1994) and through population studies conducted at medical screenings (Baron-Cohen et al., 1996). Videotapes of first birthday parties showed that children who were later diagnosed with autism were less likely to point, show objects to others, look at other people's faces, and turn toward a person calling their name than children who did not have any developmental delays. Since this was a retrospective study, none of the parents were aware that their children had autism at the time that the videotapes were made. Similarly, at 18-month medical visits, children who were later diagnosed as autistic failed to point out objects of interest (however, they could point to make a request), did not follow another person's gaze, and were unable to engage in pretend play. The presence of all three symptoms were indicative of autism. Children who were able to follow another person's gaze but failed to point and/or failed to engage in pretend play were later diagnosed as having a language delay but not autism. The similarities between these two completely different approaches to studying early signs of autism are remarkable and suggest that two symptoms in particular, not using a point to share an interest with another person and not looking at another person's face or gaze, are early symptoms that are specific to autism. Pretend play does not typically develop until 14 months of age, and therefore is not an appropriate indicator of developmental problems until 18 months. While most children are not referred for an evaluation until after 2 years of age, when their language delays are most apparent, these studies clearly show that some symptoms of autism are present and can be recognized in the first 2 years of life.

Associated Characteristics

DSM-IV lists several characteristics that are associated with autism but are not included in the diagnostic criteria. These features commonly occur in people who have autism, but they do not represent defining characteristics of the disorder. People with autism commonly show uneven cognitive patterns, often performing better on nonverbal, visual–spatial tasks than verbal tasks. Associated behavioral symptoms include hyperactivity, attention problems, impulsive behavior, aggressive behavior, self-injury, and temper tantrums. Some people with autism have odd or extreme responses to sensory stimuli such as a high pain threshold; hypersensitivity to light, sound, or touch; and fascination with certain visual or auditory stimuli. People with autism may have abnormal eating behavior (extremely limited food preferences) or disturbed sleep cycles. Also, affect may be inappropriate or flat at times. Fearfulness or, conversely, a lack of fear in situations that would normally scare others is often present. Finally, higher-functioning individuals with autism may develop depression in adolescence and adulthood as they come to recognize their differences from other people.

DIAGNOSTIC TOOLS

The diagnosis of autism should be based on multiple sources of information, including parent interviews and behavioral observations. There are several rating forms, structured play sessions, and structured parent interviews that have been developed to help the clinician diagnose autism. Several of these instruments are discussed in this section.

Childhood Autism Rating Scale

The Childhood Autism Rating Scale (CARS) (Schopler, Reichler, & Renner, 1988) is a behavior rating scale that can be completed by the child's teacher, parent, or therapist. The child's behavior in 15 different areas (e.g., social relatedness, nonverbal communication, verbal communication) is rated on a four-point scale ranging from age-appropriate behavior to severely abnormal behavior. Diagnostic classifications are made by adding up the scores for the 15 different areas. When compared to expert clinical judgments based on interviews with parents and their child, the CARS demonstrates good criterion validity ($r = .80$). An advantage of this behavioral rating scale is that it can be completed by a variety of different individuals who are familiar with the child and does not require an extended structured observational period. It also includes associated features of autism such as unusual sensory responses and fears. A disadvantage of this rating scale is that the addition of associated features means that the total score does not directly correspond to the DSM-IV diagnostic criteria.

Autism Diagnostic Observation Schedule

The Autism Diagnostic Observation Schedule (ADOS) is a standardized semi-structured play session that allows the examiner to observe communicative and social behaviors that are associated with autism (Lord et al., 1989). The examiner administers eight different tasks designed to assess the child's turn-taking, symbolic play, nonverbal, and conversation skills. The ADOS is appropriate for use with children from 6 to 18 years of age with a mental age of at least 3 years. The ADOS requires 20–30 minutes to administer. A diagnosis is made based on scoring an algorithm that is consistent with the current DSM-IV criteria. The ADOS is most effective when used along with a parent interview. In particular, questions about the child's restricted and repetitive interests are needed to supplement the information obtained from the play session in order to make a valid diagnosis. When parent information is combined with the ADOS, criterion validity is quite good. Specifically, 37 out of 40 children diagnosed with autism based on clinical judgment were also diagnosed with autism based on the ADOS and a parent interview about restricted interest (Lord et al., 1989).

Prelinguistic Autism Diagnostic Observation Schedule

The Prelinguistic Autism Diagnostic Observation Schedule (PL-ADOS) was developed as an alternative to the ADOS to use when a child is less than 6 years old and has not yet developed phrase speech (DiLavore, Lord, & Rutter, 1995). It is a semistructured 30-minute play assessment consisting of 12 activities assessing reciprocal social interaction, imitation, pretend play, turn-taking, ability to offer comfort to another person, and requesting skills. A diagnosis is made based on an algorithm that is consistent with the current DSM-IV and *International Classification of Diseases*, tenth edition (ICD-10) criteria. Compared to clinical judgment, the PL-ADOS correctly diagnosed 16 out of 18 nonverbal children with autism and 40 out of 42 developmentally disordered children without autism. The PL-ADOS is less valid when used with children who have developed phrase speech. The benefit of both the ADOS and the PL-ADOS is that these provide a brief semistructured observational format that focuses on behaviors associated with autism and is reliable with the current DSM-IV and ICD-10 diagnostic systems.

Parent Interview for Autism

The Parent Interview for Autism (PIA) (Stone & Hogan, 1993) is a structured interview for gathering information from the parents of children under the age of 6. Parents are asked to rate the frequency of behaviors associated with autism on a five-point scale ranging from never to almost always. The interview contains 118 items and requires 30–45 minutes to administer. The main use of the interview is to elicit clinically relevant information needed to determine if a child meets criteria for a DSM diagnosis. Although there are no cutoff scores to determine if a child's score is indicative of a diagnosis of autism, the total score on the PIA is moderately correlated with the CARS ($r = .42$) and with the previous edition of the *Diagnostic and Statistical Manual*, the DSM-III-R (American Psychiatric Association, 1987) ($r = .49$). One benefit of the PIA is that it allows the examiner to gain a perspective across time and different contexts in the child's life.

Autism Diagnostic Interview

The Autism Diagnostic Interview-Revised (ADI-R) is a standardized, semistructured parent interview that can be used to assess children and adults with a mental age of 18 months and up (Lord, Rutter, & Le Couteur, 1994). The interview lasts approximately 1½ hours for a child who is 3–4 years old and longer for an older child or adult. Caregivers are asked to describe their children's past and current behaviors with a focus on the behaviors observed during the preschool years. A diagnosis is made based on scoring an algorithm that is consistent with DSM-IV and ICD-10 criteria. The ADI-R has good criterion validity, with 24 out of 25 clinically diagnosed autistic children meeting criteria for autism on the ADI-R. Also, 23 out of 25 mentally retarded children without autism were diagnosed accurately as not being autistic by the ADI-R. Although the ADI-R requires a lengthy interview, to date it is the instrument that is the most consistent with our current diagnostic criteria.

HISTORY OF THE DEFINITION OF AUTISM

Although autism was first described by Leo Kanner in 1943, it did not appear in the American Psychiatric Association (APA) diagnostic series until 1980, when it was included as Infantile Autism in the third edition of the *Diagnostic and Statistical Manual* (DSM-III) (APA, 1980). Earlier definitions were offered by Rutter (1978a) and the National Society for Autistic Children (NSAC) (Ritvo & Freeman, 1977). Rutter's definition, among the first to gain wide acceptance, incorporated Kanner's insightful description of the disorder with the subsequent research, resulting in criteria that accurately blended research findings with practical experience. Like the NSAC definition, Rutter stipulated social and communication impairment with an early onset as the basic characteristics of autism. Rutter added the criterion of unusual behaviors, which he evaluated relative to developmental level. Unlike contemporary definitions, the NSAC definition added unusual sensory behaviors to the characteristics of autism.

More recent APA definitions of autism incorporate the earlier work of Kanner, Rutter, and NSAC. In DSM-III, autism was called Infantile Autism; in DSM-III-R and DSM-IV, it is called Autistic Disorder. Excluding "infantile" from the label eliminates the suggestion that autism is exclusively a childhood disorder. Although it is still believed that the onset of autism typically occurs during infancy or childhood, it is now accepted that children do not "grow out" of autism. People with autism certainly improve as they grow older, some dramatically, especially if they receive competent support and education, but they continue to need some form of assistance for the rest of their lives. A 1985 study assessing the outcomes of 14 adult men with autism (Rumsey, Rapoport, & Sceery, 1985) verified this conclusion. Although several of the men were higher-functioning and even held jobs, all of the men remained impaired, chiefly in terms of social functioning, affect, thought processes, motor habits, and language. Their levels of adaptive functioning, especially in the areas of self-direction, socialization, and occupational achievements, were quite low relative to their levels of intelligence. These adults with autism often behaved inappropriately socially, thought concretely, perseverated on topics and ideas, and engaged in stereotypic hand movements and body rocking.

Because one cannot "grow out of" autism, the category "residual autism" was eliminated in DSM-III-R. A diagnosis of residual autism was originally intended to describe people who still showed minimal signs of autism upon reaching adulthood. The symptoms that adults with autism manifest, however, are not simply remnants of their earlier impairments. Rather, an adult's symptoms represent the same impairments he or she has had since the onset of autism, altered by developmental change. For instance, social impairment in autism can be manifested in different ways at different ages. As an infant, the person with autism may stiffen when picked up, fail to cuddle, and avoid eye contact. In preschool, the same person may cling fearfully to a parent, especially in unfamiliar settings. By school age, the person with autism may begin to seek out social interaction for pleasure, but in an odd manner; for example, all conversations may begin with the same question. Finally, as an adult this person may monopolize conversations with his own preferred topics or have trouble maintaining intimate relationships.

In DSM-III-R the number of possible symptoms from which one could draw to make a diagnosis of autism increased; the increase was from six criteria in DSM-III to 16 in DSM-III-R. Consequently, the DSM-III-R definition is much broader than the DSM-III definition (Volkmar, Cicchetti, Bregman, & Cohen, 1988), resulting in more people being diagnosed with autism who had not previously met criteria for this diagnosis. The greater number of criteria is consistent with the understanding that there is a range of clinical manifestations of autism. People with autism constitute a heterogeneous group. The thoroughness of DSM-III-R, therefore, decreases the possibility that clinicians unfamiliar with autism will incorrectly diagnose patients who are at a higher developmental level. On the other hand, DSM III-R increased the chances of overdiagnosing autism (Hertzig, Snow, New, & Shapiro, 1990).

The task force appointed by the APA to develop DSM-IV endeavored to strike a balance between sensitivity and specificity. They wanted to lower the rate of false-positive diagnoses without raising the rate of false-negative diagnoses. Of all the diagnostic systems assessed by the task force, the draft version of the ICD-10 achieved the best balance of sensitivity and specificity over a range of ages and developmental levels (World Health Organization [WHO], 1990). For this reason, the task force aimed to make the new DSM-IV compatible with ICD-10. To do this, they included three new Pervasive Developmental Disorders (PDDs) in DSM-IV, as ICD-10 had done: Rett's Disorder, Childhood Disintegrative Disorder (CDD), and Asperger's Disorder. By including these new diagnostic labels, the task force intended to more accurately cover the range of syndrome expression in the Pervasive Developmental Disorders. The diagnostic criteria for autism in DSM-IV are based on those in ICD-10, with low-frequency or redundant criteria eliminated so the list of criteria is shorter and less detailed (Volkmar et al., 1994). A child must meet six of 12 DSM-IV criteria to receive the diagnosis.

The use of the term "qualitative impairment" rather than "quantitative impairment" (which denotes absence or delay) sets autism apart from other diagnoses, such as Mental Retardation and Learning Disorders. Qualitative impairment allows for deviance rather than absence, a distinction in autism often misunderstood and frequently needing emphasis. A behavior that was formerly absent or delayed, such as social interaction, may later appear in a deviant state; that is, people with autism are not always unresponsive to others, but sometimes abnormally responsive. For this reason, people unfamiliar with autism may expect to walk into a classroom of children with autism without being noticed or approached. On the contrary, the visitor may not be ignored; rather, some children with autism will make social overtures to a stranger by approaching her and touching her hair or asking her birth date. Although these behaviors are inappropriate, they represent social overtures. Similarly, language is not always absent in autism, but is often deviant. For example, a person with a good vocabulary may nevertheless have trouble understanding sarcasm and idioms, fail to use or understand gestures in speech, and speak in an abnormally high pitch. Although about half of all people with autism never develop communicative language, many children develop some speech after a delay. Even though their speech is no longer absent, it may be impaired by echolalia, pronoun reversals, or idiosyncratic phrases.

Autism as a Pervasive Developmental Disorder

As late as the 1970s, autism was considered by some to be a psychotic disorder. Indeed, it was included as such in ICD-9 (WHO, 1978). Including autism as a developmental disorder in DSM-III, in the same category as learning disorders, was a major step forward. By the 1980 publication of DSM-III, research had firmly established autism as an organic condition, with symptoms present from a very early age. DSM-III acknowledged greater similarities between autism and such disorders as Mental Retardation and Developmental Reading Disorder rather than with emotional disorders such as Overanxious Disorder. Since DSM-III, autism has remained classified as a PDD. The other disorders included with autism under this label have been Childhood Onset Pervasive Developmental Disorder (COPDD) in DSM-III, Pervasive Developmental Disorder Not Otherwise Specified (PDD-NOS) in DSM-III-R and DSM-IV, and CDD, Asperger's Disorder, and Rett's Disorder in DSM-IV.

Although the PDD umbrella has continuously appeared in the APA diagnostic series since 1980, several researchers question its appropriateness. Proponents of the PDD umbrella argue that the term was originally chosen to reflect the impairment of development "over a range of different domains" (Volkmar & Cohen, 1991, p. 1171). Volkmar and Cohen argue that the impairment in autism is pervasive because the symptoms "pervade and affect virtually every area of activity and development" (p. 1171). Mental Retardation, on the other hand, is a specific developmental disorder, in that cognitive functions are the primary impairments. For example, people with Down's syndrome often have adequate social and communicative functioning for their mental ages. Opponents of the PDD umbrella argue that, on the contrary, severe-profound mental retardation is the most pervasive of the developmental disorders (Baird et al., 1991). Autism, especially at the higher-functioning level, can be argued to represent a specific deficit in social-cognitive functioning. Many areas of functioning, such as rote memory, visual-motor skills, and self-help skills, are often spared. The term "pervasive" implies severity, which is the most variable aspect of autism (Happé & Frith, 1991). For example, it is inappropriate to say that Temple Grandin, who not only lives on her own but also has a successful career as a professor and consultant, has a pervasive developmental disorder (Grandin & Scariano, 1986).

In addition to the question of the term's appropriateness, there is the potential for damage from the PDD-NOS diagnosis (Baird et al., 1991). Autism, as a recognized disorder, commands a high level of public awareness today, but the general public is much less familiar with the term "PDD." People diagnosed with PDD-NOS may be denied services because of this unfamiliarity (Baird et al., 1991), and many professionals argue that Autism Spectrum Disorder would be a more familiar, accurate, and appropriate umbrella term than PDD (Happé and Frith, 1991).

Despite the strong arguments against the PDD label, it appears in DSM-IV. Volkmar and Cohen (1991) maintain that stronger evidence is necessary to demonstrate that the disorders under the PDD label represent different manifestations of the same underlying vulnerability before the name can be changed.

EPIDEMIOLOGICAL DATA

Prevalence

DSM-IV lists the prevalence of autism at two to five cases per 10,000 people. Epidemiological studies report a wide range of figures, with some reporting as low as two cases per 10,000 and others as many as 11.6 per 10,000 (Gillberg, 1984; Gillberg, Steffenburg, & Schaumann, 1991). There are many factors that lead to this discrepancy in prevalence figures. One confounding factor in prevalence studies is the sampling method. Not all studies actually investigate the total population. Some prevalence studies look for people who have already been diagnosed with autism or who seem to have similar difficulties by contacting clinics, hospitals, and schools. These studies may find a lower prevalence of autism because of a failure to detect people who have not sought services for autism or who have been misdiagnosed.

Secondly, because there have been many different sets of diagnostic criteria for autism and researchers have not yet agreed upon one definition, different prevalence studies have used different diagnostic systems. As a result, studies using narrow criteria find fewer cases, and those using broader criteria find more cases. Different researchers also have different ideas about what constitutes "autism" and fail to distinguish between the classic, Kanner-type autism and autism as defined by using the full spectrum of the definition of the disorder.

Are Cases of Autism on the Rise?

Some researchers suggest that recent estimates of the prevalence of autism are higher than ever because there has been a rise in the actual number of cases of autism (Ornitz, 1989; Gillberg et al., 1991). Gillberg et al. noted that in one area of western Sweden, the number of cases had risen from four per 10,000 in 1980 to 7.5 in 1984 to 11.6 per 10,000 in 1988. They attributed this rise, in part, to better detection of autism resulting from the construction of a new diagnostic center, but also to the immigration of large numbers of families to Sweden from economically depressed countries. Children of these families may be more likely to suffer from genetic disorders exclusive to their native regions, intrauterine infections, or pre- or perinatal brain damage due to inadequate medical facilities.

Arguing that demographic factors do not entirely account for the increased prevalence of autism, Ornitz (1989) hypothesized that there may actually be more children with autism in the world because of increased fetal salvage made possible by improved medical technology. Ciranello (1995) speculated that autism might be one of the genetic disorders that intensifies over generations. Citing the identification of more mild, or high-functioning, cases of autism recently, Ciranello sees the detail-oriented, highly focused, and somewhat socially odd people of the past generation as more likely to have children with autism today. Others postulate that environmental pollutants might be causing a higher incidence of autism today, although their evidence to date is weak. Whatever the cause, it does seem that there are more people with autism today, especially those functioning at higher levels intellectually and in language skill, and the increase cannot be accounted for solely by better identification methods.

Prevalence in Siblings

The 1989 UCLA–University of Utah epidemiological study reported that autism is 215 times more likely to occur in siblings of people with autism than in the general population (Ritvo, Jorde, et al., 1989). Still, the chance that each sibling born after the child with autism will develop the disorder is only 8.6%. Interestingly, these researchers found that if the first child with autism is a boy, the chance of each sibling born after that child having autism is 7%. If, on the other hand, the first child with autism is a girl, the recurrence risk in siblings is 14.5%. The investigators suggested that genetic counseling for parents who have already had a child with autism should be strongly encouraged. An early observation that children with autism are usually first-born children (Rimland, 1964) was supported in the UCLA–University of Utah study. This trend, however, was significant only in families with two children and was not found in larger families.

Sex Ratios

DSM-IV states that autism is four to five times more likely to occur in males than in females. Lord and Schopler (1987) conclude that the best estimate of the sex ratio in autism is three or four boys to every one girl. Almost all behavior disorders, mental disabilities, and learning disorders affect boys more often than girls. Therefore, it is not the direction of the gender imbalance in autism that is unusual, but rather its size. Recently, researchers noted that, although autism is more frequent in males, it is more severe in females (Lord & Schopler, 1987). The difference between the genders in autism, however, is more complicated than this statement implies. Lord and Schopler indicated that there is unlikely to be a linear relationship between the sex ratio and IQ. Rather, in comparing males and females with autism, it seems that there is an excess of females who have IQs in the mentally retarded range. Ritvo, Freeman, et al. (1989) reported an overall sex ratio of 3.7:1. Among subjects with IQs higher than 70, the ratio was 6.3:1, and among subjects with IQs lower than 50, the ratio was 2.7:1. These figures corroborate the Lord and Schopler finding that females are more highly represented in the lower ranges of intelligence.

One explanation for this phenomenon is that males show greater genetic variation on most measurable characteristics (Wing, 1981), so males with autism would be more likely to vary in severity than would females, and the range of functioning among males would be higher. Wing presented an interesting hypothesis that incorporates suggested constitutional (or perhaps environmentally determined) differences between the genders. Researchers in the field of sex differences have suggested that, among all children, girls more often excel in language, whereas boys excel in visual-spatial skills. If this is true, then boys would be more likely to compensate for the severe language impairment in autism with visual-spatial skills. Girls, however, once affected with autism, would not have this recourse, and thus would be unable to compensate. If the ratio of boys to girls with good visual-spatial skills is high, then the ratio of boys to girls with autism using them will be high also. The gender difference in the expression of autism is an exciting area of research that will benefit from further attention and could teach us more about the nature of the disorder.

Mental Retardation

Gillberg (1984) reported that 23% of people with autism have IQs above 70 in the normal or near-normal range of intelligence. The remaining 77% have mental retardation in addition to autism. Gillberg found that 50% of people with autism have IQs between 50 and 70 and that 27% have IQs below 50. These figures have been corroborated by several other studies.

Social Class Distribution

Kanner observed that the parents of his patients with autism were remarkable for their high socioeconomic status (SES) and intelligence. Later clinicians noted the same phenomenon in their patients (Cantwell et al., 1979; Rank, 1949). Although this fueled psychoanalytic arguments that parents of those with autism were likely to be obsessive and coldly intellectual, empirical data has shown that social class bias is an artifact of referral factors. Using a more valid epidemiological design than the earlier studies on clinic samples, Wing (1980) found no difference in social class among fathers of children with autism, those of children with mental retardation, and the general population. When she examined the social class of fathers whose children were seen in an outpatient clinic for children with autism and fathers who joined NSAC, she did find that it was higher than that of her comparison groups and the general population, suggesting that there is a bias toward parents with higher SES becoming more involved in parent support groups.

Studies that directly examined this sampling bias further support Wing. Schopler, Andrews, and Strupp (1979) measured possible sources of bias in their sample and found that four variables accounted for the social class differences they found: early age of onset, long distance traveled for treatment, limited availability of services, and very detailed history of their child's development. Their interpretation was that families with lower SES had less knowledge of developmental milestones, and therefore noticed difficulties in their children later. Also, these families could not afford treatment, which was often at private and specialized clinics, and therefore their children were more likely to be misdiagnosed with something other than autism. Furthermore, families with low SES were less likely to have home movies and keep records of their children's development, so they were often excluded from research studies because of insufficient information about their child's history.

Tsai, Stewart, Faust, and Shook (1982) assessed social class differences in a sample that was free from the biases noted by Schopler et al., (1979), and found none. They concluded that social class bias is in fact an artifact of referral factors. They also observed that as interest in autism grows and services increase, referral biases are disappearing. As evidence, they pointed out that most studies finding social class biases were performed before 1970, whereas most studies finding no biases were performed after 1970. This trend, suggesting that services are becoming available to all who need them regardless of income level, is encouraging.

DIFFERENTIAL DIAGNOSIS

Autism and Other Pervasive Developmental Disorders

Besides Autistic Disorder, there are four other PDDs: Rett's Disorder, CDD, PDD-NOS, and Asperger's Disorder. Although these disorders are similar enough to fall under the same diagnostic umbrella, there are firm distinctions among them. Because three of these diagnoses are new to DSM-IV, further research is necessary to educate professionals about differential diagnosis.

Rett's Disorder has been observed only in females, in sharp contrast to autism, which is at least four times more common in males. Rett's Disorder is defined by normal development, at least until age 5 months, followed by head growth deceleration between 5 and 48 months of life, loss of purposeful hand skills that were previously acquired, and poorly coordinated gait and trunk movements. Severely impaired expressive and receptive language development is characteristic of this disorder, and hand-washing movements and hand-wringing are distinctive stereotypies. Although preschoolers with Rett's Disorder may show a similar social impairment to that seen in autism, these difficulties are usually less severe than problems arising from their profound mental retardation and loss of motor skills.

In CDD, also known as Heller's Syndrome, children experience a regression in development after at least 2 years of normal development. In contrast, symptoms of autism are usually noted within the child's first year. This loss must occur before the age of 10 years in at least two of the following areas: expressive or receptive language, social skills, bowel or bladder control, play skills, or motor skills. Prior to the loss of skills the child must exhibit age-appropriate social communication and play skills. Following this loss of skills the disorder is not distinguishable from autism.

The diagnosis of PDD-NOS is used when children show impairments in social or communicative functioning or show repetitive behavior but have a later age of onset or atypical or subthreshold symptomatology. Children said to have "atypical autism" would be diagnosed with PDD-NOS.

The differences between Asperger's Disorder and higher-functioning autism are less clear-cut. Asperger's Disorder was described as "autistic psychopathy" by Hans Asperger in 1944 (Asperger, 1991). It was not until 1981, when Lorna Wing published her influential article "Asperger's Syndrome: A Clinical Account," that English-speaking researchers began to explore the syndrome. Since that time, researchers have debated about whether autism and Asperger's Disorder are distinct from one another (Volkmar, Paul, & Cohen, 1985) and, if so, how to distinguish them.

Asperger himself thought that the children he described were different from those he eventually read about in Kanner's work, in that they were: (1) not so disturbed, (2) more intelligent, (3) endowed with special abilities, (4) had a later onset, and (5) started grammatical speech earlier (Asperger, 1979). These differences are also enumerated in the ICD-10 (WHO, 1990).

More recent authors believe that there are enough clinical differences between the two syndromes to continue using the term "Asperger's syndrome," but that the two disorders differ in severity rather than symptom presentation (Ozonoff, Rogers, & Pennington, 1991; Szatmari, Bremner, & Nagy, 1989). Factors that have recently been suggested to be more common in Asperger's

Disorder than in autism are: motor clumsiness (Wing, 1981), a higher family history of Asperger's Disorder (Szatmari et al., 1989), and a higher occurrence of circumscribed interest patterns (Kerbeshian, Burd, & Fisher, 1990).

DSM-IV differentiates the two disorders by stipulating that people with Asperger's Disorder do not show a delay in language development. However, there is evidence that this differentiating factor should not be uncritically accepted and that language development in Asperger's Disorder is far from normal. Whereas Asperger placed great emphasis on the impressive-sounding speech of his patients, Wing (1981) did not believe that their speech is unimpaired. She found that the content of their speech sounds like an imitation of something heard or read, and it often seems to have been learned by rote. Asperger (1991) described their speech as like that of an adult. The speech of people with Asperger's Disorder often sounds pedantic with inflection lacking or, at the least, unusual. It may be difficult for them to start or continue a conversation, and when they do engage in one they cannot tailor their topic to the social context. They tend to speak only for a purpose and do not "chat" (Szatmari, 1991). Further clinical experience and research will help establish the validity of Asperger's Disorder as a distinct syndrome.

Autism and Mental Retardation

Although many people with autism have the additional diagnosis of mental retardation, the two disorders are distinct from one another; there are people with autism who do not have mental retardation and people with mental retardation who do not have autism. The two disorders share the primary characteristics of a lifelong course and impaired intellectual ability. Also, several symptoms occur in both disorders: echolalia, self-stimulatory and self-injurious behavior, delayed symbolic play, and attention problems. The language and social abilities of people with mental retardation, however, are usually limited only by their intellectual abilities. That is, children with mental retardation seek affection in a manner appropriate for children of their mental age, whereas children with autism seek affection in unusual ways, such as backing into their parents' lap or asking repetitive questions. Language and social impairments are central characteristics of autism and are present to a marked degree even in people of normal intelligence. Furthermore, people with mental retardation typically show a consistent impairment across a wide range of functioning.

For people with autism, cognitive abilities are more scattered; many people with autism exhibit unique patterns of cognitive strengths and weaknesses usually resulting in IQ profiles characterized by peaks and valleys. Also, people with autism more commonly have normal physical development (Schreibman, Loos, & Stahmer, 1993), while children with mental retardation are often delayed in reaching motor milestones. Fine motor impairments, however, are common in autism. Neurological abnormalities appear earlier in mental retardation than in autism. In severe mental retardation, seizures begin in infancy; in autism, they usually do not occur until puberty. The neurological abnormalities in autism are more subtle and varied than in mental retardation (Phelps & Grabowski, 1991). Also, physical abnormalities are rarely noted in people with autism.

Autism and Learning Disabilities

Superficially, it seems that differential diagnosis between autism and learning disabilities should be relatively easy, but there are similarities between the two groups. The social awkwardness of children with learning disabilities and the uneven cognitive skills often present in autism narrow the discrepancies between learning disabilities and higher-functioning autism (Cox & Mesibov, 1995). Both groups have intelligence levels above the borderline range of intellectual functioning. Similarly, both groups often show large discrepancies among learning functions in that the same child may be severely delayed in one area and superior in another. These groups also share language problems, difficulties in interpersonal functioning, and cognitive disorganization. Social interaction can be as problematic for children with learning disabilities as it is for children with autism, although the specific skill deficits might differ between the two groups. Children with learning disabilities often have low social status at school, with few friends and unsatisfactory social interactions. In a like manner, children with autism may also experience low social status in the school environment because they have difficulty understanding the more subtle aspects of social interactions, such as responding to nonverbal and affective cues. Shea and Mesibov (1985) suggest that the social difficulties in both disorders may be closely linked to the children's language comprehension deficits. Finally, in the area of cognitive disorganization, both groups of children need structured settings to help with their difficulties in sequencing and planning and to reduce their distractibility and impulsivity.

The similarities between higher-functioning autism and learning disabilities have often led to misdiagnoses; many people who are diagnosed with autism for the first time in young adulthood were considered learning disabled throughout their school years. In general, autism is the more severe disorder, with more peculiar behaviors. People with autism are more impaired and deviant in interpersonal relatedness, communication, and behavior. Children with autism have more severe social deficits and more difficulty at every step of social interaction. These children often appear odd to others and typically are unaware of their impact on others. On the other hand, children with learning disabilities are painfully aware of their social failures, appearing more awkward and immature than odd.

Whereas all children with learning disabilities can communicate and comprehend others in some way, about one-half of children with autism cannot functionally communicate. Those children with autism who can communicate have peculiar language behaviors such as echolalia, pronoun reversal, odd prosody, and use of rote phrases and questions.

Behavior problems of children with learning disabilities can be linked to their social and communication impairments and to impulsivity. In autism, however, behavior problems are more peculiar and severe, consisting of self-injurious behavior and self-stimulation, rigid adherence to routines, and resistance to change.

Autism and Attention Deficit Disorder

Parents and teachers often report that children with autism have attention problems. In fact, some children who are eventually diagnosed with autism are brought to professionals with attention problems as the primary concern. Like children with Attention Deficit Disorder (ADD), children with autism may seem not to be listening when they are directly addressed, appear to be "spacy," have difficulty following verbal instructions, and problems concentrating in school.

Children with autism commonly have shorter attention spans than would be expected for their age. Although people with autism share features with people with Attention Deficit Disorder (ADD), the underlying reasons for these symptoms are different. A main factor behind attention problems in autism is mental retardation. Often, the attention span of a child with autism is appropriate for his mental age, rather than his chronological age, so a 12-year-old child with autism who is functioning at the 2-year-old intellectual level would understandably also have the attention span of a 2-year-old. This would explain a high activity level and a tendency to quickly become bored with toys or activities.

The social and communicative impairments that define autism can also result in attention difficulties. Children with autism may not attend to adults' verbal directions or comments because of their aloofness or because they are more interested in something else. These children may not attend to or process verbal stimuli because of difficulty with receptive language. Attention problems in autism are discussed in more detail in Chapter 4.

In addition to these explanations, three groups of researchers have offered theories on the nature of attention in autism. First, Lovaas and his colleagues outlined the stimulus overselectivity theory (Lovaas, Koegel, & Schreibman, 1979) to account for children's problems in learning and in generalizing learned material. Lovaas et al. suggested that when presented with multiple stimuli, people with autism only respond to a limited number of stimuli or to part of a stimulus; thus, when listening to a lecture in school, the child with autism may attend to the teacher's hand movements, rather than to what is said. Lovaas et al. were able to apply this theory to language and emotional impairments as well as learning impairments, although stimulus overselectivity was found not to be specific to autism (Gersten, 1980).

Frith (1989) proposed a theory that is related to the stimulus overselectivity theory, but allows for the fact that some people with autism are not overselective. She suggests that people with autism are able to attend to multiple aspects of a cue, but often choose to attend to a narrow, idiosyncratic aspect rather than an aspect that people without autism would immediately find salient. Her theory is that salience and context are different for people with autism. Frith cites the failure of people with autism to take account of context to illustrate her theory. The example she gives is the strength that people with autism show on puzzles, and therefore on the Object Assembly subtest of the Wechsler Intelligence Scale for Children (WISC) (Rutter, 1983). Frith and Hermelin (1969) demonstrated that even children with autism who have severe mental retardation are able to successfully construct puzzles using the shapes of the pieces, rather than the picture, as a guide. For them, the shape is more meaningful than the picture.

This ability, or disability, is also exhibited in Tager-Flusberg's (1991) study of word memorization. When presented with a list of words to memorize, the performance of people with autism was the same, regardless of whether or not the words were related to one another. People without autism are able to use the context of the related words to aid memory. Additionally, Courchesne and colleagues (1994) suggested that people with autism might have difficulty shifting their attention. Once a person with autism is attending to something (e.g., a person's hairstyle), they have difficulty shifting their attention to another, perhaps more important, piece of information (e.g., the person's facial expression). This could explain why it is difficult to get the attention of a person with autism and why they have difficulty understanding the many aspects of social interactions.

Autism and Obsessive-Compulsive Disorder

Stereotypies in autism often appear quite similar to the rituals performed by people with Obsessive-Compulsive Disorder (OCD). Also, the restricted interests of persons with autism (e.g., weather, dates) often resemble obsessions. Usually, however, the stereotypies in autism are simpler than the rituals in OCD. For example, a person with autism may rock back and forth or repetitively rub his lips; OCD rituals usually take the more complex form of cleaning or checking (Sturgis, 1993).

Another discriminating factor is ego-dystonia. People with OCD, incapacitated by their rituals, desperately want to be free of them. This is not the case in autism, as the awareness of how nonproductive and debilitating the rituals and obsessions can be is much more limited (Swedo & Rapoport, 1990). Finally, people with OCD rarely show the mental retardation, speech defects, and severely impaired relationships that are present in autism.

Autism and Developmental Language Disorders

Because one of the three areas impaired in autism is language, children with autism share many symptoms with children who have difficulties and delays in the comprehension and vocal expression of language. These include echolalia, pronoun reversal, sequencing problems, and difficulty with comprehension (Phelps & Grabowski, 1991).

In contrast to children with autism, however, children with language disorders maintain eye contact, communicate with gestures, share their interests and accomplishments with others, and are emotionally responsive. Riguet, Taylor, Benaroya, and Klein (1981) reported symbolic play impairments in both children with autism and children with developmental language disorders. The play of the children with autism, however, was impaired below their language mental age. In contrast, children with language disorders displayed pretend play skills that matched the level of their language mental age. Also, many of the deficits shown by children with language problems are rarely seen in autism: errors in articulation, omission of crucial words, and choosing incorrect words.

Rutter (1978b) used the link between autism and what he called Developmental Receptive Aphasia (DRA) as support for his theory that autism is primarily a disorder of language. He found cases of both disorders appearing in different children in the same family. Perhaps some genetic predisposition for language difficulties was being expressed differently by different siblings. The two groups of children shared several symptoms, as well as a negative correlation between language skill and autistic-like social and behavioral characteristics.

Although Rutter postulated that autism and DRA were both disorders of language that frequently appeared in the same families, he clearly distinguished between them by the more readily apparent problems of social functioning and behavior in autism. Rutter also detailed specific differences in use of language. First, children with autism showed a more severe deficit in the comprehension of language. Also, they were poorer at understanding gestures. Second, the language impairment in autism was more extensive, affecting not only spoken language and gestures, but also written language, sequencing, and abstraction. Third, whereas both groups of children had delayed language, language in autism was just as deviant as it was delayed. In DRA there are few language abnormalities. The more typical manifestation of this disorder is severe language retardation. Finally, Rutter noted that children with autism used their language skills poorly. In contrast, the children with the language disorder used what skills they had satisfactorily even though their skills were reduced.

Autism and Schizophrenia

In his original description of the disorder, Kanner (1943) distinguished autism from childhood schizophrenia. He pointed out that autism was present from the beginning of the child's life, whereas schizophrenia was preceded by at least 2 years of normal development. In autism, the child showed signs of the disorder from early infancy; in schizophrenia, there was a change in behavior preceded by normal development.

Kanner felt that two other differences between the disorders made them distinct: Children with autism did not develop hallucinations, as children with schizophrenia did, and children with autism had less history of psychosis in their families than did children with schizophrenia. However, Kanner believed that the social isolation present in both disorders linked them. He concluded that autism and childhood schizophrenia were different disorders, but that autism was the earliest manifestation of adult schizophrenia. Autism, Kanner believed, should be included as a subgroup of the schizophrenias (Eisenberg & Kanner, 1956).

Despite Kanner's distinction, in the years following the similarities between the two disorders led researchers and clinicians to use the two labels interchangeably. Indeed, the two disorders share some symptoms: social difficulties, resistance to change, speech abnormalities, and constricted or inappropriate affect (Schreibman et al., 1993).

Eugen Bleuler (1950) further linked the two disorders, including "autism" as one of the "four As" that formed the core symptoms of schizophrenia. Bleuler coined the term "schizophrenia" in 1911, over 30 years before Kanner coined the term "early infantile autism." Bleuler used the narrowest, most concrete meaning of "autism," defining it as "the splitting of a person's relationship with reality, leading to dominance of the inner life" (Carson & Sanislow, 1993). Of course, the current use of the term is much broader, describing a syndrome rather than an isolated symptom.

Today, with the accumulation of much evidence distinguishing them, autism and schizophrenia are viewed as completely separate disorders. Rutter (1968) presented evidence not only that autism and child schizophrenia are separate, but also that autism and adult schizophrenia are unrelated. Rutter pointed out that the sex ratios of the two disorders were strikingly different; autism affects males four times as often as females; schizophrenia, however,

Table 2.2. Differential Diagnosis

	Mental retardation	Learning disabilities	Schizophrenia
Characteristics shared with autism	Lifelong course Impaired intellectual ability Shared symptoms: echolalia, self-injury, self stimulation, attention problems	Social awkwardness Uneven cognitive abilities Language problems Cognitive disorganization Need for structure	Social difficulties Resistance to change Speech abnormalities Constricted or inappropriate affect
Differentiating features	Language and social abilities limited only by intellectual abilities Consistent impairment across wide range of functioning Abnormal physical development Delayed motor milestones Neurological abnormalities appear earlier	Impairment generally less severe All develop communication methods Behavior problems are less severe and less peculiar	Onset later in life Hallucinations present History of psychosis in family more common Affects both genders equally Mental retardation rare Remissions and relapses, rather than steady course

affects both genders equally. Also, he noted that mental retardation is very common in autism, but rare in schizophrenia. And, whereas the course of autism is steady, the course of schizophrenia is characterized by remissions and relapses.

Schreibman et al. (1993) noted that people with schizophrenia often evidence poor motor development and health, which is uncommon in those with autism. Although both disorders are characterized by language deviance, people with schizophrenia, unlike those with autism, always acquire language (Phelps & Grabowski, 1991) (see Table 2.2).

SUMMARY

Since Kanner first coined the term autism in 1943 professionals have struggled to define the disability clearly and functionally. In 1981, autism was officially recognized by DSM-III, representing a major advance in these efforts. Over the past 15 years, the definition has been refined to acknowledge the lifelong nature of the disability, its subtleties, and its essential features, including early onset, social problems, communication difficulties, and narrow interests and resistance to change.

Better definitions of autism have improved identification procedures and also the accuracy of epidemiological data. Autism resembles and overlaps with many related disorders, including Mental Retardation, Learning Disabilities, ADD, OCD, Developmental Language Disorders, Schizophrenia, and other PDDs. It is important to understand the overlaps, similarities, and differences between autism and these related conditions.

Current Biological Theories of Causation

Today it is commonly accepted that autism is a neurobiological disorder that is present at birth or develops within the first 30 months of life. After almost two decades of research, the precise causes of autism remain unclear. The research on biological causes of autism has been fraught with contradictory and disappointing results; findings are rarely replicated and often do not add up to a coherent explanation. There are several clues concerning the underlying brain dysfunctions in people with autism, however, and the methods by which these brain dysfunctions may be transmitted. These clues will be discussed in this chapter.

GENETIC FINDINGS

Genetic research has provided some of the strongest evidence that autism is a biological disorder. Same-sex twin studies have compared the concordance rates of autism between monozygotic and dizygotic twin pairs. If genes are completely accountable for autism, one would expect a 100% concordance rate for autism in monozygotic twins. That is, since both twins share the same genetic code, they would both be expected to have autism any time one of them has the disorder. In contrast, among dizygotic twins who do not share identical codes, the expected concordance rate for autism would be similar to the concordance rate among all siblings.

Several epidemiological same-sex twin studies have examined the genetic component involved in autism. Across these studies, concordance rates for autism in monozygotic twins have ranged from 36% to 91% (Bailey et al., 1995; Folstein & Rutter, 1977; Steffenburg et al., 1989). Not a single pair of dizygotic twins were concordant for autism in any of these studies. The fact that these studies showed a much greater concordance rate among monozygotic twins strongly suggests some genetic factor underlying autism. Because the concordance rate for monozygotic twins is less than 100% in all of the studies, however, we can also assume that genetics alone cannot be responsible for autism.

Data from family studies examining the rate of autism among siblings also suggest a genetic component to the disorder. The prevalence of autism is about 1 per 1000 and the risk of having a second child with autism is approximately 3–8%. Although a 3–8% risk is still small, it is substantially greater than the prevalence of autism in the general population (Smalley, Asarnow, & Spence, 1988). The chance of having a second child with any of the PDDs after having one child with autism has been estimated between 5 and 7% (Bolton et al., 1994; Szatmari, Jones, Tuff, Bartolucci, Fisman, & Mahoney, 1993). If the pervasive developmental disorders followed a dominant-recessive inheritance pattern, the rate should be 25%. Thus, while family and twin studies strongly support an underlying genetic etiology in autism, it is not a dominant or simple straightforward genetic pathway.

Any theory about the genetic abnormality underlying autism must account for the heterogeneity of the disorder. Individuals with autism can have very different clusters of symptoms that might range from mild to severe. For example, one child with autism can have mental retardation and mutism and may actively avoid interacting with others. In contrast, another child with the same autism diagnosis may have above-average intelligence and fluent speech and may actively seek friendships, albeit oddly.

There are two different genetic theories that seek to account for the heterogeneity seen in autism. First is the notion that there may be a more general genetic abnormality that impairs cognitive and social functioning, with autism representing a particularly severe form of this genetic problem. This theory can help account for the different levels of severity seen in people with autism. Second, there may be a variety of genetic disorders that cause autism, each characterized by a slightly different array of symptoms, but all leading to the impaired social relationships, communication skills, and perseverative behaviors characteristic of the disorder. Each of these theories is reviewed in this section.

Is Autism a Severe Form of a Genetic Disorder Causing Social and Cognitive Impairments?

Twin and family studies support the notion that autism may result from a single gene abnormality that can be manifested by varying levels of severity. For example, monozygotic twins who both have autism can differ in the types of autistic symptoms displayed and in their IQ scores. A recent study by Le Couteur et al. (1996) has shown that monozygotic twins can have IQ scores that are up to 50 points apart. Additionally, among monozygotic twins not concordant for autism, the nonautistic twin often has some of the impaired cognitive and/or social skills found in autism (Bailey et al., 1995). In contrast, among dizygotic twins, there are no reports of both twins having autism, and it is rare (10%) for the nonautistic twin to have cognitive and/or social impairments.

Family studies also show a link between autism and other cognitive and social abnormalities in first-degree relatives (Bolton & Rutter, 1990; Rutter, MacDonald, Le Couteur, Harrington, Bolton, & Bailey, 1990). Specifically, 15–25% of siblings of autistic children are reported to have some form of cognitive abnormality. A link for reciprocal social impairments in family members has also been found. Bolton and Rutter report that 12% of autistic children's siblings had impaired social interactions. In comparison, no siblings of Down's syndrome children had trouble with social skills. These cognitive and social difficulties appear to persist throughout adulthood, are less severe than the impairments observed in classic autism, and are rarely associated with mental retardation. These findings strongly suggest a single gene disorder may cause developmental impairments for social and cognitive skills. There may be a broad range of abnormalities that can result from this type of genetic disorder. If a person has a significant level of impairment in these skills, then they are given the diagnosis of autism.

Szatmari et al. (1993) have questioned the notion of a single gene abnormality causing a wide range of social and cognitive impairments. They found that siblings of children with autism who had cognitive or social problems could be diagnosed as having one of the other PDDs. If all siblings with PDDs were excluded, siblings of autistic children did not differ from siblings of children with Down's syndrome. Thus, they argue against the hypothesis of a genetic link to a broad phenotype of social-cognitive abnormalities and instead propose a narrower phenotype encompassed by the diagnosis of one of the PDDs. Although less broad, their data still suggest that there are several social and cognitive disorders that may be caused by a single genetic abnormality.

Currently, there is no explanation for why some members of a family have autism while others have a less severe cognitive-social impairment. Bailey, Phillips, and Rutter (1996) proposed a "two-hit mechanism" in which one set of causal factors predisposes a person to a broad array of cognitive-social disorders and a separate set of causal factors is involved in the transition to the more serious disorder of autism. This second set of causal factors could be either an additional genetic abnormality or an environmental event (e.g., a prenatal insult).

Is Autism Caused by Several Different Genetic Abnormalities?

The fact that autism co-occurs with known single gene disorders such as fragile X syndrome, phenylketonuria (PKU), and tuberous sclerosis supports the notion that autism may be a single disorder that can be caused by multiple gene abnormalities. The relationship between each of these disorders and autism is reviewed in this section.

Fragile X

Fragile X is a constriction of the long arm of the X chromosome and is characterized by enlarged testicles, a long face, and large ears. Usually, but not always, mental retardation and hyperactivity are present. It occurs in approximately 1 in 1250 males and 1 in 2500 females and in 5–10% of individuals with mental retardation.

Social and language impairments are associated with fragile X, and some individuals with fragile X also meet criteria for a diagnosis of autism. Reports vary widely on the comorbidity of these two disorders, with estimates ranging from 0 to over 50%. Reiss and Freund (1990) examined the rates of autistic behavior in a group of 17 males with fragile X. They reported that three (17.6%) men met criteria for autistic disorder and that 10 (58.8%) men met criteria for some type of pervasive developmental disorder other than autism. In their study, the subset of autistic symptoms displayed by individuals with fragile X included poor peer interactions, abnormal verbal and nonverbal communication, stereotypic motor behavior, and unusual responses to sensory stimuli. In contrast, the fragile X group did not show some of the core symptoms of autism because most were aware of others' emotions, sought comfort appropriately, demonstrated good imitation skills, developed language, and were not unduly upset by changes in routine. Although several of these individuals technically met criteria for a diagnosis of autism, it is unclear if they should be considered "autistic" because they do not have some of the core symptoms associated with the disorder. While Reiss and Freund stated that low IQ in fragile X individuals was not associated with increased autistic behavior, others have argued that the overlap between fragile X and autism can be accounted for by the symptoms of mental retardation that are present in both disorders (Dykens, Leckman, Paul, & Watson, 1988).

Another way to look at the overlap between fragile X and autism is to examine the number of autistic people who also have fragile X. Again, estimates vary widely ranging from 0 to 20%. More recent studies use strict diagnostic criteria for both autism and fragile X and yield more consistent findings ranging from 2.4 to 2.7% (Bailey et al., 1993; Payton, Steele, Wenger, & Minshew, 1989; Piven, Tsai, Nehme, Coyle, Chase, & Folstein, 1991). This rate is less than the rate of fragile X found in people with mental retardation and suggests that the overlap between autism and fragile X may be accounted for by the overlap between autism and mental retardation.

In summary, although the comorbidity of fragile X and autism is well-documented, there is some controversy about the extent of this overlap and whether the large majority of autistic individuals with mental retardation may account for the overlap. The fact that a single gene disorder, such as fragile X, is more often found in autistic individuals with mental retardation than autistic individuals without mental retardation suggests that perhaps mental retardation and not autism is associated with fragile X.

Phenylketonuria

PKU is an inability to break down the amino acid phenylalanine that is present in many common foods. It is usually, but not always, associated with the gradual development of mental retardation, occurs in 1 in 14,000 births, and is inherited via an autosomal recessive pathway. Routine testing for PKU is conducted on all newborns in the United States, and mental retardation can be prevented through a phenylalanine-free diet.

PKU was one of the first genetic disorders thought to be associated with autism. Prior to the development of the screening test, children with untreated PKU were noted to show symptoms associated with autism, including poor social skills, mutism, and repetitive behaviors. Dietary treatment was found to be effective in reducing these autistic symptoms but not in treating the mental retardation. It is interesting to note that the relationship between autistic-like symptoms and PKU does not appear to be caused by mental retardation because the autistic-like symptoms can be ameliorated without changing the level of retardation. It is unclear whether these children would have met current diagnostic criteria for autism. Ethically, it is not possible to withhold treatment for children with PKU, and therefore the link between autism and untreated PKU cannot be verified through the use of current and more reliable diagnostic methods.

Tuberous Sclerosis

Tuberous sclerosis is a neurocutaneous disorder characterized by mental retardation, seizures, skin lesions, and intracranial lesions. It is an autosomal dominant disorder that occurs in 1 in 7000 births. There have been multiple reports about the association between autism and tuberous sclerosis. Estimates of the rate of autism among children with tuberous sclerosis have been as high as 50%. Hunt and Shepherd (1993) report that 24% of children with tuberous sclerosis in their study met criteria for autism, and an additional 19% showed some symptoms of autism. Interestingly, only children with mental retardation and tuberous sclerosis showed autistic symptoms. Using standardized diagnostic measures of autism, Smalley, Tanguay, Smith, and Gutierrez (1992) showed that seven out of 18 individuals (39%) with tuberous sclerosis met criteria for autism. Six out of the seven were also severely retarded. Although there appears to be a clear link between tuberous sclerosis and autism, tuberous sclerosis cannot account for the majority of cases of autism. Only 0.5–3% of autistic individuals have tuberous sclerosis.

Other Genetic Disorders

Gillberg et al. (1991) presented a series of case studies in which autistic children had a partial trisomy of chromosome 15. The fact that this abnormality was identified in multiple individuals with autism suggests that further examination of the relationship between autism and partial trisomy of chromosome 15 is warranted. There have been other case studies reporting the presence of some type of genetic abnormality in an autistic person. Other than the data on the fifteenth chromosome, however, these case studies have not been replicated.

Summary

In summary, there is a great deal of evidence supporting the notion that autism is a genetic disorder; however, the particular chromosomal impairment remains unknown. It is unclear whether autism is caused by a single genetic abnormality or whether it can occur from a number of different genetic abnormalities. The most convincing evidence suggests that there may be a genetic link to a variety of cognitive and social abnormalities, with autism being the most severe form. Current research is focusing on families with multiple persons with autism in an attempt to isolate the gene or genes that are responsible for these cognitive and social abnormalities. Until this information is available, it is difficult to offer specific information in genetic counseling to families having a relative with autism. When counseling families about the chance of having a second child with autism, however, it is important to note that while the risk is low (i.e., 1–3%), there is a greater probability of having a second child with a milder form of cognitive and/or social skills impairment (i.e., 10–25%).

PRENATAL AND PERINATAL COMPLICATIONS

Two factors suggest that there may be an environmental, as well as genetic, link to autism. First, because monozygotic twins are not always concordant for autism, there may be an additional environmental insult that leads to one twin having autism but not the other. Second, if there is a genetic abnormality that causes social and cognitive impairments, then there must be an additional factor that determines whether the impairments will be mild or severe. It has been hypothesized that pre- and perinatal complications, when combined with a genetic predisposition, may lead to the development of the severe social and cognitive abnormalities that characterize autism.

Compared to their siblings and normally developing control children, children with autism do have more pre- and perinatal complications. It has been hypothesized that increased complications are linked to mental retardation rather than autism per se. A recent study of children with autism who are not severely retarded, however, has shown that their mothers also have increased rates of pregnancy complications (Lord, Mulloy, Wendelboe, & Schopler, 1991). Therefore, mental retardation cannot completely account for the link between autism and pre- and perinatal problems.

Unfortunately, the literature has been contradictory and few specific pregnancy complications have been corroborated across multiple studies. The most common problems reported by mothers of autistic children are increased maternal age (greater than 35 years), bleeding after the first trimester, use of prescription medication, meconium in the amniotic fluid, and gestational period longer than 42 weeks (Lord et al., 1991; Tsai, 1987). It is important to note, however, that many women have these complications during pregnancy without having a child with autism. Similarly, many mothers of autistic children do not experience these, or any other, complications during pregnancy. While many women believe that a particular pre- or perinatal complication is responsible for their child's autism, currently there is no proof that any specific complication causes autism.

An environmental factor that is associated with autism is birth order. Autistic children are more likely to be born first in two-child families or fourth or later in families of four or more children. Some authors have argued that the preponderance of first-born autistic children is because parents with one autistic child often decide not to have more children once they receive the diagnosis. Additionally, researchers have argued that during their first pregnancies mothers are more likely to work in the community and thus be exposed to viral illnesses, while during later pregnancies, mothers may be exposed to their school-aged children's infectious diseases. Viral illnesses during pregnancy, however, have not been consistently associated with autism. Whatever the cause, this birth order phenomenon has been one of the most robust and puzzling findings reported in the literature on pre- and perinatal complications associated with autism. It would be interesting to examine whether there are more complications during first pregnancies in which the child develops autism compared to first pregnancies in which autism does not occur.

NEUROANATOMICAL FINDINGS

Researchers have theorized that autism may be caused by abnormalities in brain development. Through the use of magnetic resonance imaging (MRI), computerized tomography (CT) scanning, autopsy studies, and animal models, several different areas of the brain have been implicated. Recent research has demonstrated abnormalities in three areas of the brain: the cerebellum, the limbic system, and the cerebral cortex. In addition, there has been some evidence suggesting an overall enlargement in brain size in autism rather than a specific localized impairment. The research suggesting anatomical abnormalities in each of these areas is reviewed in this section.

Cerebellum

The cerebellum is connected to systems regulating attention, sensory modulation, and motor and behavior initiation. In addition, the cerebellum is thought to be linked to emotion-modulation and language-processing systems. Each of these systems has been theorized to be impaired in individuals with autism.

Support for anatomical abnormalities in the cerebellum of autistic individuals comes from autopsy and MRI studies. Autopsies have been conducted on relatively few autistic individuals, and therefore the findings should be interpreted with caution. Two different research groups have reported autopsy results indicating a reduced number of Purkinje cells in the cerebellar hemispheres (Bauman & Kemper, 1988; Ritvo et al., 1986). MRI studies have corroborated the autopsy findings. Courchesne and colleagues reported that the cerebellar vermal lobes VI and VII are considerably reduced in size in persons with autism (Courchesne, Yeung-Courchesne, Press, Hesselink, & Jernigan, 1988; Hsu, Yeung-Courchesne, Courchesne, & Press, 1991). The majority of the participants in the MRI studies had intellectual abilities within the average range, indicating that the cerebellar cell loss (or hypoplasia) does not appear to be caused by the mental retardation that often accompanies autism.

It is believed that the cerebellar hypoplasia is caused by a lack of development during the prenatal period (most likely during the late second and early third trimesters of pregnancy) rather than an atrophy following a period of normal development. This theory has been supported by two sets of findings. First, the cell loss has been observed in young children with autism (Hashimoto, Tayama, Murakawa, & Yoshimoto, 1995). Presumably the fact that this anatomical abnormality is present early in life indicates that a degeneration did not occur, and instead the abnormality is present from birth. Second, if a period of normal development was followed by a degenerative process, one would expect that the degeneration would be caused by abnormal anatomical pathways leading into or out of the cerebellum. Instead, the cell loss seems specific to the cerebellum (Hsu et al., 1991).

Although these findings of cerebellar cell loss have been exciting and led some to hope that the underlying cause of autism had been found, this biological marker does not appear to be present in all individuals with autism. In fact, several researchers have reported no cerebellar abnormalities in MRI (Kleiman, Neff, & Rosman, 1992) and positron emission tomography (PET) studies (Heh et al., 1989). These discrepant findings may be because of the characteristics of the autistic individuals studied, such as age and intellectual functioning. Also, abnormal cell loss in the cerebellum may be related to the epilepsy that co-occurs in some persons with autism rather than the autism per se. There have been a few autopsies conducted on individuals without a history of seizures, however, who still showed evidence of cerebellar damage. It may be that cerebellar cell loss is present in a particular subgroup of autistic individuals characterized by such factors as age, intellectual development, and epilepsy.

Limbic System

The social skill deficits observed in individuals with autism have been theorized to reflect abnormal functioning in the limbic system. Bachevalier (1994, 1996) has developed an animal model of autism that supports the theory that limbic system impairments may be involved in autism. Specifically, she found that monkeys with lesions in the medial temporal lobe (amygdala and hippocampus) exhibited autistic-like behaviors, including failure to develop normal social relationships, blank facial expressions, poor body language, lack of eye contact, and motor stereotypies. Interestingly, the social withdrawal seemed to worsen with time. At 2 months of age the monkeys were passive but did not actively withdraw from social contact. By 6 months of age, the monkeys actively withdrew from the social initiations of other monkeys. This finding is particularly intriguing when compared to reports by parents of preschoolers with autism who describe a gradual deterioration in their children's social and language skills. Bachevalier's research provides an animal model for both the unusual behaviors observed in individuals with autism and the development of the disorder during the early years of life.

There is some empirical evidence for limbic system abnormalities in persons with autism. Autopsy studies have revealed reduced neuronal cell size and increased cell-packing density (increased numbers of neurons per unit volume) in portions of the limbic system (i.e., the hippocampal complex, subiculum, entorhinal cortex, amygdala, mammilary body, medial septal nucleus, and anterior cingulate gyrus) (Bauman & Kemper, 1985). It is not known if the limbic system damage occurred during pre-, peri-, or postnatal development. In contrast to the autopsy studies, a recent MRI study has not found any evidence of abnormalities in the hippocampus (Saitoh, Courchesne, Egaas, Lincoln, & Schreibman, 1995).

Human research studies to date have not identified specific subgroups of individuals with autism who have hippocampal and/or amygdala abnormalities.

The animal model research has noted, however, that the severity of autistic symptoms in monkeys is associated with the level of limbic system impairment. When the amygdala and hippocampal regions are lesioned separately, early damage to the amygdala seems to play a greater role in creating autistic-like symptoms than early damage to the hippocampus. The most severe autistic-like behaviors, however, have been observed in monkeys with damage to the amygdala, hippocampus, and adjacent cortical areas. Bachevalier (1994, 1996) suggested that in persons with high-functioning autism the amygdala may be more affected than the hippocampus. In contrast, both the amygdala and hippocampus, as well as surrounding cortical areas, may be affected in cases of severe autism accompanied by mental retardation. This is one of the few anatomical findings that provides an explanation for the wide range of severity associated with autism and future research with human subjects needs to be conducted to corroborate this theory.

Cerebral Cortex

The cerebral cortex regulates higher-order cognition, including language, abstract reasoning, and planning. Because each of these abilities is impaired in autism, it has been hypothesized that abnormal development of the cerebral cortex may be an underlying causal factor in autism. Surprisingly, in the past few years, only two MRI studies have been published citing cerebral cortex damage in persons with autism. First, Piven and colleagues found cortical malformations (i.e., polymicrogyria, macrogyria, and schizencephaly) that were located in a variety of different brain locations in both hemispheres (Piven, Berthier, Starkstein, Nehme, Pearlson, & Folstein, 1990). They hypothesized that these types of malformations resulted from a defect in the migration of neurons to the cerebral cortex during the first 6 months of prenatal development. Because their subjects did not have mental retardation, their data cannot be attributed to the mental retardation that often accompanies autism. While these findings suggest that autism may be associated with global developmental problems in the brain, the lack of specificity makes it difficult to theorize how this type of impairment would lead to the specific set of behaviors observed in autism. This finding needs to be replicated in order to verify the connection between cerebral cortex abnormalities and autism.

Second, Courchesne, Press, and Yeung-Courchesne (1993) noted parietal lobe abnormalities in 43% of the persons with autism in their study. The same pattern of parietal lobe cell loss was not present in each person. Parietal lobe abnormalities included cortical volume loss, white matter loss, and a thinning of the corpus callosum near the parietal lobe. The individuals with parietal lobe damage showed the same type of selective attention impairments observed in nonautistic adults with acquired parietal lobe damage (e.g., stroke, tumor). Courchesne and colleagues suggested that pre- or perinatal damage to the cerebellum may cause aberrant signals to be sent to the parietal lobe during its development. These aberrant signals could cause the nonspecific altered neuron growth in the parietal lobe that they found. Although this hypothesis is intriguing, it is important to note that over half of the individuals with autism in this study did not show any parietal lobe abnormalities. Perhaps this finding characterizes a specific subgroup of individuals with autism. Based on a single research study, this theory about parietal lobe abnormalities needs to be verified in future investigations.

Brain Size

Several researchers have noted an increase in total brain volume in some individuals with autism (Piven, Arndt, Bailey, Havercamp, Andreason, & Palmer, 1995). In normal brain development, there is an overgrowth of neurons that are pruned during the first few years of life. It has been theorized that the large brain size in autism may indicate that this normal pruning does not occur in some individuals with autism (Minshew, 1996). As with the data on cerebral cortex abnormalities, this finding of global brain impairment in autism does not readily suggest why the specific social, language, and cognitive impairments observed in autism result from this abnormality.

Summary

Minshew (1996) summarizes the literature on neuroanatomical research in autism as an apparent contradiction between findings suggesting too little brain development and findings suggesting too much brain development. That is, some researchers suggest a lack of neuronal development (e.g., findings of cerebellar hypoplasia, decreased neuronal cell size in the limbic system, polymicrogyria in the cerebral cortex, and decreased volume in the parietal lobe), while other researchers suggest an overgrowth of neurons (e.g., findings of increased density of neurons in the limbic system, macrogyria in the cerebral cortex, and increased overall brain weight).

Although these findings may seem to contradict each other, taken together they suggest a single theory about the underlying cause of autism. That is, autism may be caused by abnormal cell growth during the early stages of brain development. In normal brain development, neurons proliferate and become interconnected, gradually reducing in size and number once certain connections become more heavily utilized than others. It is this process of neuronal growth and pruning that seems to be abnormal in autism, leaving some areas of the brain with too many neurons and other areas with too few neurons. The vast majority of studies suggest that this process goes awry during prenatal development and persists throughout the early years of life as the brain continues to develop. The exact cause of this type of abnormality remains unknown and is perhaps associated with the genetic abnormalities or prenatal insults discussed earlier in this chapter.

Whether this abnormal neuronal growth is specific to certain areas of the brain or is more global in nature is also unknown. Certainly the research on the cerebellum and the limbic system strongly points to specific abnormalities in these areas. While we have made tremendous progress in understanding the neuroanatomic abnormalities associated with autism, more research clearly is needed.

CORTICAL ELECTROENCEPHALOGRAPHIC FINDINGS

EEG studies have been conducted to clarify the nature of cortical impairments in individuals with autism. In general, EEG studies have provided information about two separate topics: (1) abnormal patterns of neuronal activity across different brain locations, and (2) abnormal levels of brain activity (seizures).

Patterns of Brain Activity

Patterns of brain activity can be analyzed in several different ways. First, the left and right hemisphere of the brain are specialized for different skills and it is possible to examine whether the pattern of left and right hemisphere activity in autism is similar to the pattern seen in normally developing persons. Second, EEG analyses can examine the activity level of different regions of the brain (e.g., frontal, temporal, and parietal lobes) as a way of ascertaining whether cortical impairments are localized to certain regions of the brain or are more global in nature.

Hemispheric Lateralization

At birth, each cortical hemisphere is lateralized for specific functions. The pattern of hemispheric lateralization appears to be abnormal in persons with autism, suggesting that autism is associated with cortical brain impairments. Early theories of abnormal hemispheric laterality in autism came from research on hand dominance suggesting that there may be an increased rate of left-handedness (controlled by the right hemisphere) in autism (see Chapter 1 for a review). Other support for abnormal hemispheric laterality in autism comes from examining performance on tasks believed to require either left or right hemisphere processing. Usually, verbal communication skills involve left hemisphere processing, while visual-spatial tasks involve right hemisphere processing. Individuals with autism have poor verbal skills that are associated with left hemisphere functioning and good visual spatial skills that are associated with right hemisphere functioning.

Dawson and colleagues (Dawson, Warrenburg, & Fuller, 1983) used EEG techniques to further examine the relationship between left and right hemispheric laterality in autism. They found that, in contrast to the expected pattern, individuals with autism showed greater right than left hemisphere activation during language and motor imitation tasks (another traditionally left hemisphere skill). They displayed the typical right hemisphere dominance pattern for spatial tasks.

The data on abnormal hemispheric laterality in autism can be interpreted in several different ways. The abnormal hemispheric laterality may reflect underlying damage to the left hemisphere leading to poor performance on left hemisphere tasks (e.g., language and motor imitation) and decreased right-handedness. Findings that some right hemisphere abilities are impaired in persons with autism (e.g., understanding emotional expressions), however, suggests that more than left hemisphere impairment is involved in autism.

Dawson and colleagues propose that the abnormal hemispheric laterality pattern present in autism reflects an underlying right, not left, hemisphere abnormality. They state that the right hemisphere is overactive and prevents the left hemisphere from developing its traditional lateralized role. This theory is supported by the finding that, in persons with autism, the right hemisphere seems most affected by language development (Dawson, Finley, Phillips, & Galpert, 1986). Specifically, children with the least developed language ability showed the most increased right hemisphere activation. Also, greater language ability was not related to increased left hemisphere activity, but instead was related to decreased right hemisphere activity. Dawson and Lewy (1989b) suggest that the increased right hemisphere activity may be a result of an impairment in cortical-subcortical neuronal connections (e.g. in the cortical-limbic-reticular system loop). This theory is supported by the anatomic findings discussed earlier of abnormal cell numbers in both the limbic (hippocampus and amygdala) and the cortical (parietal lobe) systems.

Regardless of which theory is correct, these findings show that the functioning of the cerebral cortex is impaired in autism. More work needs to be done in examining whether the abnormal hemispheric lateralization in autism changes with age and whether it characterizes a particular subgroup of individuals with autism.

Activity Level across Brain Regions

A recent study by Dawson, Klinger, Panagiotides, Lewy, and Castelloe (1995) found support for the theory that several different cortical regions of the brain function abnormally in autism. Compared to normally developing children matched on receptive language mental age, children with autism showed increased neuronal activity in the frontal and temporal lobes, but not the parietal lobe. The authors point out that the frontal and temporal lobes are the two cortical regions that are most closely linked to the limbic system and that their findings are consistent with theories of abnormal limbic system development in autism (see the MRI and autopsy studies discussed earlier in this chapter). These findings do not support the MRI results of Courchesne and colleagues (Courchesne et al., 1993) suggesting parietal lobe impairment in autism.

Interestingly, Dawson and colleagues found evidence of subgroup differences in brain activity levels for persons with autism. Subgroups were defined by their social behavior: One group of children passively engaged in social interaction only when approached by another person; a second group of children was less socially impaired, actively approaching and engaging in social interaction. The children with the most social impairments (the passive group) demonstrated increased brain activity levels in the frontal region compared to normally developing children matched on both chronological age and receptive language mental age. The autistic children with more developed social skills did not show this difference in brain activity level. This is one of the first findings of biological differences in subgroups of autistic individuals and suggests that social impairments in autism are linked to frontal lobe abnormalities. This exciting result needs to be replicated in future research.

Taken together, EEG studies examining patterns of brain activity in different hemispheres and regions of the brain indicate that there are global cortical impairments in autism. Evidence suggests that there may be impairments in the frontal and temporal regions of the brain across both the left and the right hemispheres of the brain.

Seizure Disorders

The increased rate of abnormal EEGs and seizures in autism compared to the general population further supports the theory of global cortical impairments in autism. It is estimated that between 20 and 30% of individuals with autism develop seizures before the age of 18 years. Although it is unclear why some individuals with autism develop seizures and others do not, there are a few factors that are associated with a dual diagnosis of seizures and autism.

One of the clearest patterns is for seizures to occur more frequently in autistic individuals who have mental retardation. Volkmar and Nelson (1990) reported that 81% of individuals with both autism and seizures have an IQ score of less than 50. In comparison, 58% of autistic individuals without seizures have an IQ score of less than 50. Second, two recent studies found some preliminary evidence suggesting that females with autism may be at higher risk for developing seizures than males with autism (Elia, Musumeci, & Ferri, 1995; Volkmar & Nelson, 1990). This finding may be an artifact of the fact that females with autism tend to be more severely retarded than males. Therefore, the higher rate in females may simply be another piece of evidence supporting the fact that seizures are more linked to mental retardation than to autism per se.

Earlier research suggested that seizures were not the cause of autism, but rather, were developed subsequent to the onset of autistic symptoms. This theory was supported by Deykin and MacMahon's (1979a) report that seizures often develop during adolescence rather than early childhood. More recently the research suggests that there may be two common periods when seizures are most likely to develop: prior to 3 years, and during puberty (11–14 years). Volkmar and Nelson (1990) hypothesized that the earlier age of onset may be related to pre- and perinatal complications while later onset may result from the biological changes that occur during puberty in an already at-risk population.

Clinically, autism is not associated with one particular type of seizure. Generalized tonic-clonic seizures (e.g., major motor seizures), complex partial seizures, and absence seizures (i.e., staring spells) have all been observed in individuals with autism. The lack of specificity again supports the notion of global cortical abnormalities in autism.

Landau–Kleffner Syndrome

Recently, the news media has highlighted a possible link between autism and a specific seizure disorder, Landau–Kleffner syndrome. Landau–Kleffner syndrome, also known as acquired aphasia with convulsive disorder, is characterized by a progressive loss of the ability to understand language and use speech following a period of normal speech development. It is accompanied by seizure activity and is typically diagnosed through a sleep EEG (Gordon, 1990; Pacquier, Van Dongen, & Loonen, 1992). Stefanatos, Grover, and Geller (1995) have recently published a case study describing a child with Landau–Kleffner syndrome. They reported that treatment with corticosteroids resulted in improvements of language abilities and behavioral disturbances (e.g., hyperactivity, tantrums, poor social skills, motor stereotypies). They concluded that in cases where Landau–Kleffner syndrome and autism co-occur, pharmacological treatment may be effective in treating the autism. These findings must be viewed cautiously as there has only been one case study published to date. Certainly there have been many cases in which children with autism have appeared to develop language normally and then showed regression. It is unclear, however, whether this phenomenon is the same as that experienced by individuals with Landau–Kleffner syndrome.

Summary

Individuals with autism have abnormal cortical functioning that is apparent from a wide range of EEG studies examining lateralization of specific skills across different brain hemispheres, patterns of activation across different regions of the brain, and seizure activity. In general these studies suggest that there is not one specific area of the cortex that is abnormal in autism, and instead the impairments are more global in nature. These impairments may indicate abnormal development of the connections between subcortical (e.g., the limbic system) and cortical areas of the brain.

NEUROCHEMICAL FINDINGS

Researchers have examined a variety of neurochemicals (e.g., serotonin, dopamine, norepinephrine, endogenous opioids) in their search for the underlying cause of autism. To date no biochemical marker for autism has been found. Although individual studies have implicated each of these neurochemicals in the etiology of autism, findings have not been consistently replicated. Even double-blind, placebo-controlled, carefully conducted studies have failed to replicate one another.

This lack of consistent results has been disappointing and leads to several different interpretations. First, it is possible that there truly is no biochemical marker for autism and the few significant findings are because of chance rather than any true effect. Second, it is possible that there are neurochemical markers for autism, but that these markers cannot be consistently found by measuring peripheral (e.g., blood and urine tests) levels of the neurochemicals. Instead, measurement of central levels through analysis of cerebrospinal fluid and actual brain concentrations (e.g., through postmortem brain tissue analyses) may yield more conclusive findings. Third, it may be that neurochemical markers are present in specific subgroups of individuals with autism. Factors such as level of mental retardation, family history, and level of social impairment may all be important in determining which, if any, subgroup of autistic individuals have abnormal neurochemical functioning.

Across all of the different studies, there are two neurochemicals that have been most strongly implicated in the etiology of autism: serotonin and endogenous opioids. Even though the findings for these two neurochemicals are inconclusive, they warrant further discussion.

Serotonin

One of the most consistent findings in the neurochemical literature is that individuals with autism have elevated peripheral (whole blood) levels of serotonin. This elevation is caused by an increased level of blood platelet uptake or storage of serotonin. Serotonin has been implicated in the behavioral-physiological processes of sleep, pain and sensory perception, motor function, appetite, learning, and memory. It is possible that the perception, learning, and memory impairments found in persons with autism may be associated with this increased level of serotonin. No consistent relationship between level of serotonin and level of behavioral impairments, however, has been reported.

It has been hypothesized that reducing the level of serotonin may reduce behavioral impairments in persons with autism. A multicenter study of fenfluramine, a stimulant medication that reduces peripheral levels of serotonin, yielded inconclusive results. Overall, fenfluramine was not found to have a consistent effect on IQ, social responsiveness, or communication skills, but it may be effective in reducing hyperactivity among some children with autism (du Verglas, Banks, & Guyer, 1988). Increased levels of serotonin are found in persons with mental retardation, and it is unclear if the increased levels found in autism are related to a dual diagnosis of autism and mental retardation.

One study has found support for a particular subtype of autism and increased levels of serotonin. Piven, Tsai, Nehme, Coyle, Chase, and Folstein (1991) reported that serotonin levels are higher in autistic individuals with a family history of the disorder than in autistic individuals without a family history of autism. This finding was not caused by differences in sex, age, or IQ. It is possible that elevated levels of serotonin may be a marker for individuals with a genetic transmission of autism.

Serotonin has also been implicated in the process of early brain development. Ciaranello and Ciaranello (1995) hypothesized that some early abnormality in serotonin levels may disrupt the maturation of the CNS, leading to an abnormality in neuronal connections. The possibility of abnormal neuronal development and pruning was discussed earlier in the section on neuroanatomical findings, and it is intriguing to consider whether abnormal serotonin levels may underlie this phenomenon.

Brain Opioids

Endogenous opioid peptides have been implicated in the regulation of pain perception, social and emotional behaviors, and motor activity. Panksepp (1979) proposed that elevated levels of endogenous brain opioids may cause the self-stimulatory behavior and social and emotional impairments exhibited by persons with autism. To date, however, there is little empirical support for this theory. In fact, decreased levels of beta-endorphins (one type of opioid peptide) have been reported in the cerebral spinal fluid of persons with autism (Gillberg & Coleman, 1992; Sandman, Barron, Chicz-DeMet, & DeMet, 1991).

Support for the theory that there may be elevated levels of endorphins in autism comes from clinical trials of opiate antagonists (naloxone and naltrexone) that reduce levels of endorphins. Several researchers reported decreased self-injurious behavior in persons with autism who were treated with opiate antagonists. A more recent double-blind, placebo-controlled study, however, did not find any effect on the social problems that characterize autism (Campbell et al., 1993).

Summary

Currently there is no neurochemical marker that is present in every individual with autism. The literature has been fraught with inconclusive results. The only consistent findings have been the presence of elevated levels of serotonin in the blood of some individuals with autism. The relationship between elevated levels of serotonin and specific behaviors observed in autism, however, remains unclear. This finding is not specific to autism and thus may not be a true biological marker for autism. Future research in this area needs to focus on the possibility of abnormal neurochemical levels in specific subgroups of individuals with autism.

CONCLUSIONS

Although incredible progress has been made in documenting the biological abnormalities that are associated with autism, the underlying cause of autism remains unknown. Only about 10% of the cases of autism have been associated with a known medical condition (e.g., tuberous sclerosis), and the biological cause of the remaining 90% remains a mystery. There are many promising theories, however, regarding underlying etiologies of autism.

One of the most integrative current theories suggests that autism may result from abnormal neuronal growth during prenatal development. This atypical neuronal development has been hypothesized to underlie the findings of abnormal anatomical structure in the cerebellum, limbic system, and cerebral cortex, although the reasons for this neuronal cell growth are unclear. Ideas have included a possible genetic abnormality, pre- and perinatal insult, and abnormal neurotransmitter concentrations. The evidence for a genetic component to autism is particularly convincing, specifically the findings that there may be a genetic abnormality that causes a wide variety of social impairments, including autism.

It is important to note that even the most promising studies have failed to find evidence for a single abnormality that is present in every individual with autism. Even more discouraging is the fact that few findings have been consistently replicated. This lack of conclusive findings indicates that autism may be a broad diagnostic label that results from a number of different etiologies. Inconclusive results may arise when several different etiological subgroups are combined. Thus, conclusive findings will only emerge once specific subgroups have been identified.

Despite the continued mystery about the underlying cause of autism, there have been significant gains in our understanding of this disorder. It is now commonly accepted that autism is a biological disorder, we can counsel parents on the chances of their having a second child with autism or related social impairments, and we can assure them that autism does not result from poor parenting.

Language and Cognition

One of the most striking characteristics of autism is the uneven profile of language and cognitive abilities. Language difficulties among those with autism who speak are varied and often striking. They include the well-known pronoun reversals that psychoanalysts used as evidence for an identity crisis as well as the echolalia that the behaviorists so carelessly tried to extinguish. Today semantic and pragmatic difficulties in social interaction are often overlooked and misunderstood. Language difficulties are prevalent in autism and are thus important for us to examine.

Each person with autism also appears to have "peaks" and "valleys" in his or her ability to understand information. For example, persons with autism often demonstrate phenomenal rote memory skills; parents report that their child can recite lists of past events such as driving routes, weather facts, and menus read at different restaurants. Because of these peak skills it is easy to assume that the child has normal or gifted cognitive abilities.

These peak skills, however, are often accompanied by significant impairments in other areas of cognitive functioning. For example, although rote memory skills are spared, impairments in recognition memory are usually present. At times, these weaknesses are viewed by professionals and parents as refusals to cooperate. For example, because the child can stare intently at a favorite object, his lack of cooperation in attending to his name being called is considered to be willful disobedience rather than a difficulty shifting attention from one activity to the next. There has been quite a bit of research focused on understanding which cognitive functions are spared and which are impaired in autism. This chapter will focus on the weaknesses and strengths seen in language and cognitive processes.

LANGUAGE ABILITIES

One of the most consistent patterns among children with autism is significantly delayed language development. Earlier estimates were that almost 50% of individuals with autism do not develop functional and communicative language at all during their lifetimes (Rutter, 1978c). Although the figure is thought to be closer to 35–40% today, it is still substantial. Among those individuals who eventually learn to speak, there is a particular pattern of strengths and weaknesses that has been observed. Comparing preschool children with autism to a matched sample of children with Down's syndrome, Tager-Flusberg (1993) found that the main differences were in how effectively the children with autism used the language skills that they had acquired. Children with autism were not specifically impaired in their ability to pronounce words or in their ability to learn language structures such as how to construct sentences using appropriate word order. They did show difficulties, however, in the semantic aspects of language (i.e., vocabulary development and understanding word meanings) and in the pragmatic aspects of language (i.e., the social use of language).

Semantic Aspects of Language

Children with autism tend to use a limited range of words during their conversations and often don't fully use the vocabulary that they have developed. Parents frequently report that their child can say hundreds of words, but instead tends to use only a few words during his or her conversations.

In addition to their limited use of vocabulary, persons with autism have some deviant characteristics of their language such as pronoun reversal and echolalia. Pronoun reversal is characterized by referring to themselves as "you" instead of "I" and calling others "I." Investigating pronoun usage among adolescents with autism, Lee, Hobson, and Chiat (1994) observed a tendency to refer to the examiner by name rather than "you" and to themselves by name rather than "I" or "me." They noted that pronoun reversals sometimes become less severe over time, but still persist throughout the life span.

Echolalia, defined as the verbatim repetition of previously heard words or phrases, occurs in approximately 85% of children with autism who eventually develop speech (Schuler & Prizant, 1985). Although once considered by behaviorists to be an inappropriate self-stimulatory behavior, echolalia is now viewed as a way in which children with autism can communicate with others and is considered an important precursor to the development of more advanced language. Immediate echolalia is easy to identify because a phrase is repeated immediately after it is spoken. Delayed echolalia can be harder to identify because hours or even days might pass before the autistic child repeats the phrase and the person who first made the statement might no longer be present. Delayed echolalia may also occur when a child repeats a phrase from a television show or movie. Unless you have also seen the show it is often difficult to identify the phrase as echolalic. Although their ability to remember the exact wording of previously heard conversations is impressive, this type of conversation is inflexible and often inappropriate to the situation.

The language comprehension of people with autism has often been described as concrete and literal. They do not use the semantic content (or meaning) in understanding language any more effectively than in producing it. This difficulty with semantic understanding can be especially problematic for more capable people with autism. Because of their high levels of skill most people assume they understand everything that is being said to them, which is not true. Attributions for their inappropriate responses usually assume noncompliance or stubbornness, rather than their inability to understand meanings or expectations.

Pragmatic Aspects of Language

Language impairments in autism are most pronounced in the social or pragmatic use of language (Tager-Flusberg, 1989). Several aspects of the conversation skills of verbal people with autism are obviously deviant; these include use of irrelevant detail, perseveration on specific topics, inappropriate shifts to new topics, ignoring the initiations introduced by others, and lack of strategies for repair when there are problems in their conversations.

Irrelevant details frequently enter into the conversations of people with autism. They will often provide dates, ages, addresses, or telephone numbers when referring to a person as part of a social exchange. They might also add the height of mountains in feet and meters when describing a trip or the place of birth and birthday of a friend when discussing a recent visit to their hometown. Although their recall of these dates and facts is impressive, it frequently interferes with the flow of conversation.

Perseveration on specific topics is also common. Many people with autism have idiosyncratic interests that dominate their thinking and overwhelm conversational partners. Buses, airplanes, train schedules, or sports are among the topics that might be pursued to the exclusion of others. Sometimes these topics are unusual, but more often it is the single-minded pursuit of them that is most distinctive when compared to normal conversations.

People with autism frequently have trouble staying on topic, especially when topics are introduced by the other speaker. They frequently and inappropriately shift to new topics of conversation without acknowledging the other speaker's interest or perspective. Social repairs, common among normal speakers when there is a breakdown in communication, are infrequently seen in the conversations of people with autism. Their single-minded pursuit of topics that interest them from their own perspectives is a major characteristic of their conversational interactions.

Tager-Flusberg (1993) hypothesizes that people with autism do not understand the implicit rules of social conversation. Part of their problem is their inability to understand that others have perspectives different from their own. Difficulties picking up the rules of social discourse and understanding other perspectives contribute to their pragmatic deficits.

EMOTIONAL PERCEPTION AND EXPRESSION

Hobson (1992) argues that individuals with autism have difficulties in the perception and understanding of other people's emotions, and these problems, rather than communication, represent their core deficit. He has conducted several studies supporting this hypothesis. In one study he demonstrated that children with autism sorted photographs according to the type of hat being worn rather than by facial expressions. A contrasting IQ-matched group of children with mental retardation sorted on the basis of facial expression. Another study with older children showed deficits in matching photographs of facial expressions with emotionally expressive voices. This does not appear to be because of difficulties in all visual perception abilities. In fact, visual perception skills are considered a strength in autism. For example, many children with autism learn their numbers and letters before they can talk.

Several investigators and many parents and professionals have noted that children with autism display unusual emotional expressions. Laughing can occur during periods of anxiety, and people with autism might cry for no obvious reason. Studies have demonstrated that children with autism are more likely to display negative affect and unusual blends of expressions in comparison to children with mental retardation and normally developing children. Smiles combined with eye contact or in response to others' smiles are seen less frequently in children with autism.

Loveland, Tunali–Kotoski, Pearson, Brelsford, Ortegon, and Chen (1994) reported that producing affective expressions upon request is more difficult for people with autism than for those with Down's syndrome. In this study both groups could perform rote copying of facial expressions, but the children with autism had more difficulty generating appropriate expressions without a model.

The area of emotional understanding and expression is still new and not fully explored. It does seem that the complexity of human emotions is difficult for people with autism to interpret in terms of both their own emotional feelings as well as those of others. The emotion of anxiety seems to be dominant in people with autism who have difficulty interpreting more subtle emotional states. Their emotional expressions are also less consistent in reflecting and identifying underlying feelings.

Many interesting features of memory in autism have been noted. Most noticeable are their skills in the area of rote memory. Many people with autism show impressive skills in rote memory, often for material that seems unimportant and meaningless to others, such as bus schedules or royal family trees. People with autism also seem to have well-developed skills in visual memory; they rarely fail to notice when there has been even the smallest change in their familiar surroundings. Areas of memory impairment have also been noted. Boucher and Lewis (1989) hypothesize that people with autism often engage in repetitive questioning because they do not remember having asked the question or having it answered previously. They also point out the difficulty people with autism have in following spoken directions, often forgetting the direction before they are able to carry it out. Although researchers agree that rote memory is intact in autism, studies of other areas of memory have resulted in contradictory findings because of issues of diagnosis, methodology, and interpretation of results.

Over the past 2 years, memory researchers have addressed the question of whether there is a link between autism and amnesia. Persons with amnesic syndrome have normal intellectual functioning but experience extensive memory problems caused by damage to the medial temporal and diencephalic brain structures. Some researchers have found memory deficits despite normal learning in people with autism and have linked this to the amnesic syndrome. The comparison of autism to amnesia began when researchers noticed symptoms similar to autism in monkeys with temporal lobe lesions (i.e., lesions in the hippocampus and amygdala) (Bachevalier, 1994; Boucher & Warrington, 1976). These monkeys, like people with autism, had symptoms such as motor stereotypies, increased activity levels, reduced exploration of their environments, lack of facial and body language, and social withdrawal.

In amnesia, it is assumed that recognition memory (recognizing something seen before) is harder than recall (recalling without any visual cues) and that cued recall is easier than free recall. Boucher and Warrington (1976) found impaired recognition memory, impaired free recall memory, and normal cued recall memory in autism. Boucher and Lewis (1989) found that cued recall on a task of long-term memory for events varied among subjects, but that most subjects were able to remember events as well as controls when asked very leading questions. This amnesic pattern of impaired free recall and intact cued recall has been called into question by several researchers who found no impairments in autism relative to mental age-matched normally developing children on either type of task (Minshew & Goldstein, 1993). The findings of Boucher and Warrington may be caused by differences in diagnostic criteria or lack of an appropriate mental age-matched control group.

It may be possible to account for the contradictory findings in the area of memory in autism by seeing the memory deficit as a developmental lag rather than due to an amnesic syndrome. That is, people with autism may "grow out of" their memory difficulties, so that older, higher-functioning subjects show better memory skills than younger, lower-functioning ones. Indeed, normally developing children show improved recall and recognition memory abilities as they age! Minshew and Goldstein (1993) suggest that, unlike deficits in social, communicative, and cognitive functions, memory deficits in autism may be transient, tending to fade away with age. Ozonoff, Pennington, and Rogers (1991) found that verbal memory scores were strongly correlated with mental age.

Boucher (1981a,b) has consistently found that people with autism have better short-term memories for more recently presented items on a list. This recency effect holds for people without autism, but Boucher found that the effect is much stronger in those with autism. This strength often obscures differences between autistic and control subjects in experiments by making overall recall scores similar. People with autism remember more items from the end of the list than do control subjects, but control subjects remember more items from other positions in the list, especially the beginning. Boucher hypothesized that recency effects in autism come from reliance on acoustic memory and that subjects with autism fail to encode earlier-presented items. Boucher maintains that these findings support the link between autism and amnesia.

Minshew and Goldstein (1993) pointed to deficits in organization of complex information, rather than deficits in memory. It may be that people with autism seem to have memory problems, but really their problem comes during the processing that occurs before they are able to commit material to memory. Their dysfunctions might be in the areas of encoding and organization, which make it difficult for them to actually acquire information to commit to memory. This hypothesis is supported by the enhanced recency effect in autism discussed earlier. Furthermore, researchers have noted that in people with autism who have remarkable rote memories, material seems to be stored without being interpreted, changed, or applied in a meaningful way.

Research on categorization abilities lends support to the theory that there is an impairment in the way that people with autism encode new information. Normally when learning a new category (e.g., dog) we do not memorize every example we have seen (e.g., every individual dog). Instead, we abstract across different examples and form a best image or prototype. This prototype is a single summary representation. Klinger and Dawson (1995) have proposed that persons with autism may be unable to abstract information during encoding, and thus may be unable to form a prototype. They found that persons with autism could categorize when a rule defined category membership (e.g., "all dogs have long noses"). They had no problems remembering the rule. People with autism could not categorize, however, when no rule or combination of rules determined category membership. That is, they could not abstract information to form a prototype. These results suggest that the impairment may be one of encoding rather than memory per se. This deficit might help explain why people with autism have particular difficulties processing social information, as social processes are less likely to be rule governed.

To explain contradictory and surprising findings in the area of memory, investigators have often puzzled over the effects of other autistic symptoms on memory performance. Specifically, they have addressed the issue of language problems affecting memory for verbal material, making memory for verbal material inferior to memory for nonverbal material. Ozonoff, Pennington, & Rogers (1991) found that higher-functioning subjects with autism showed depressed performance on a verbal memory task and hypothesized that language and social impairments caused memory difficulties. Consistent with this hypothesis, other researchers have found normal performance on nonverbal tasks involving visual stimuli and meaningless tones (Lincoln, Allen, & Kilman, 1992).

Conversely, some researchers have hypothesized that memory problems may be partially accountable for some of the language difficulties in autism. Specifically, when people with autism have difficulty following spoken directions, this may be because they forget the directions before they are carried out. Indeed, Boucher and Lewis (1989) found that their subjects with autism were unable to follow either spoken or visually demonstrated instructions. When instructions were written (requiring verbal ability but no memory), however, the subjects had no trouble carrying them out.

ATTENTION

In school and in social interactions, children with autism may be accused of failing to pay attention or of "being in their own worlds." They may seem not to listen, which has often led parents and teachers to suspect deafness. On the other hand, the same child who may ignore loud noises that would startle other children may listen intently to, or be annoyed by, the humming of fluorescent lights. Many children with autism seem to be hyperattentive to visual stimuli, picking up bits of lint that are barely visible to others or staring intently at a reflection that is typically overlooked. This simultaneous inattentiveness and overattentiveness is puzzling and has led to several interesting theories that attempt to explain the general pattern of attention in autism.

An early and innovative theory that seemed to account for this paradox was stimulus overselectivity (Lovaas et al., 1979). According to this view, people with autism choose one stimulus in the environment as the focus of their attention to the exclusion of all others. For instance, a child may attend to a hook on the wall of his classroom, thereby failing to attend to his teacher's lesson. Dawson and Lewy (1989a) proposed that children with autism are overaroused, and thus choose one stimulus and screen out all others in order to regulate arousal. Ultimately, stimulus overselectivity was found not to be specific to autism, but rather to be related to mental retardation. However, it continues to guide theories of attention in autism.

Frith (1989) has proposed that people with autism show selective attention. That is, they attend to idiosyncratic stimuli because these stimuli, rather than others, are most salient to them. When explicitly required to attend to particular stimuli, people with autism are able to do so. When given choices, however, they consistently focus on narrow aspects of their environments. In particular, Frith proposed that children with autism focus on details rather than gestalts. Their focus on parts rather than wholes is why they can complete puzzles from turned-over pieces that only show the shape of the pieces, rather than the picture. Shah and Frith (1993) demonstrated that people with autism excel at the Block Design subtest of the WISC. They proposed that the reason for their skill is weak central coherence, or the tendency to see the designs as segmented parts rather than as gestalts. The implication of these assertions is that people with autism are not inattentive; rather, they attend to what they see as meaningful or salient. Meaningfulness and salience for them is typically a more narrow and circumscribed aspect of the environment than for normally developing people.

Courchesne and colleagues (1994) have elaborated on these theories to propose that people with autism appear overselective in attention because of an impairment in shifting attention. According to this theory, people with autism have difficulty and are slower at disengaging attention from one stimulus and shifting it to another. People without autism are able to rapidly shift attention between stimuli and from one modality to another (from seeing to hearing). People with autism seem to restrict their attention, however, perhaps because they are unable to disengage and reorient in rapid succession.

The capacity for sustained attention seems to be intact in autism, and it has been seen as both a strength and a weakness (Dawson, 1996). If people with autism show selective attention to idiosyncratic stimuli and have difficulty shifting attention, then their intact sustained attention will be focused on circumscribed and irrelevant aspects of the environment. Thus, if they attend to narrow aspects of the environment at the expense of the gestalt, they miss much of what is meaningful around them. Some researchers, however, have hypothesized that this pattern of attention accounts for savant skills in autism and may also contribute to narrow interest patterns in autism (Frith, 1989). People with autism often take such an all-consuming interest in a topic that they learn more about it than anyone else. For example, a child who devotes his attention to studying maps to the exclusion of other information may appear brilliant when asked directions to a particular location, but will seem delayed when asked about an algebraic equation or an interpretation of *The Great Gatsby*.

THEORY OF MIND

Theory of mind refers to the ability to understand that others have beliefs, desires, and intentions that are different from one's own. These concepts are firmly established in most normally developing children by age 3–4, and they have been hypothesized as a specific impairment in children with autism (Baron-Cohen, Leslie, & Frith, 1985). Theory of mind deficits could certainly explain problems that children with autism have in social understanding and communication.

In their seminal study, Baron-Cohen et al. (1985) compared the performance of children with autism, children with Down's syndrome, and normally developing children on a theory of mind task. Each child watched a puppet show in which a character placed a toy in one location and then left the room. While the puppet was away the toy was moved to a different location by a different puppet. Children were asked where the puppet who had initially been in the room would look for the toy upon her return. A correct answer requires children to understand that the puppet had more limited information than they did and would be expected to act on that information. Although a child might know that the toy had been moved, in order to demonstrate a theory of mind, he would also have to realize that the puppet did not know the toy was moved.

Normally developing and Down's syndrome children answered the question correctly from the puppet's perspective approximately 85% of the time, in contrast to children with autism, who were only correct 20% of the time. Even persons with autism without mental retardation have difficulty on this task. Recent studies (Ozonoff & McEvoy, 1994) have corroborated these findings. It appears as if there may be a ceiling on theory of mind development in autism. This theory of mind problem is not due to global impairments in perspective-taking. Persons with autism are able to describe the visual perspective of another person (e.g., using Piaget's three mountain task). The impairment seems specific to understanding that others can have a belief or intention that is different from one's own belief or intention.

Specific prelinguistic deficits, including joint attention skills (Mundy & Sigman, 1989) and imitation (Meltzoff & Gopnik, 1993), may contribute to these theory of mind impairments. Mundy and Sigman were the first to hypothesize that a major deficit in autism is the inability to share experiences with caretakers during the first years of life. This skill is thought to evolve into the understanding of others' perspectives. Lacking this early ability interferes with the understanding that others have beliefs and concepts that are different from one's own.

It has been argued that early imitative games between infants and caregivers provide another important foundation for sharing and later predicting human behavior. Meltzoff and Gopnik describe these interactions as providing children with "primers in common-sense psychology." They are a way that children can learn how their behavior affects and influences others. Imitation, it is argued, could also be a necessary precursor for the development of a theory of mind. Imitation impairments, especially imitation of body movements, are seen in children with autism (Dawson & Adams, 1984). Parents of children with autism may try to involve their children in imitative games, but children may not participate in these games because of an inability to imitate. Without these experiences, children with autism may be unable to develop a theory of mind. Imitation impairments are amenable to treatment (Klinger & Dawson, 1995). It would be interesting to see if improvements in imitation are accompanied by improvements in theory of mind.

EXECUTIVE FUNCTIONS

Executive functions are cognitive variables describing behaviors that are thought to be mediated by the frontal lobes of the brain (Ozonoff, 1995). These neuropsychological functions include planning, impulse control, flexibility of thought and action, and organized searches. Executive functioning skills require the ability to disengage from the environment or context and be guided by mental processes or internal representations.

Executive functioning difficulties were first identified in clients with visible brain damage in their frontal lobes. More recently, investigators have noted these difficulties in people with autism as well (Ozonoff, Pennington, et al., 1991). Their behavior can be inflexible and they often become distressed over minor changes in the environment. Clients with autism insist on following routines and can be perseverative, focusing on specific details, narrow interests, or repetitive stereotypic behaviors. People with autism can have trouble inhibiting responses and have large stores of information that they cannot use meaningfully.

Several studies have documented executive functioning deficits in adults (Rumsey & Hamburger, 1988) and children with autism (Prior & Hoffman, 1990). In these studies the authors noted difficulties in generating strategies or learning from mistakes. Approaching tasks such as copying were difficult for people with autism, who tended to focus on details rather than the overall figure and had difficulty initiating and generating appropriate strategies.

If ongoing research corroborates the hypothesis that frontal lobe dysfunction underlies many of the executive functioning problems of autism, this could have implications for treatment. Remediation efforts could highlight the development of specific executive functioning skills. For example, students could be taught to break tasks into steps to aid in their planning and to develop hierarchies of increasingly complex goals and sequences (Ozonoff, 1995). To help with knowledge application, teachers could emphasize identifying the main information in paragraphs and associating that with already acquired knowledge to maintain a focus on the larger picture. Other process-oriented learning strategies would be applicable as well.

SUMMARY

Individuals with autism show a puzzling pattern of strengths and weaknesses. They seem to have impairments in some aspects of linguistic and cognitive functioning but have intact abilities in other related areas. It is this uneven pattern of abilities that has most intrigued and confused parents and professionals in their attempts to understand autism. Understanding the language and cognitive abilities of people with autism is essential for the development of effective teaching strategies.

In the area of language development, people with autism who learn to talk are able to articulate words and understand grammar (i.e., rules of ordering words in a sentence) fairly well. In contrast, they tend to have trouble with semantic and pragmatic components of language; that is, they do not use the vocabulary words they know, and they have trouble using language socially to converse with other people. Treatments focused on teaching pronunciation and the development of new vocabulary words are not focused on the specific impairments in autism. Instead, treatments need to focus on initiating conversations, using a broad array of words in conversations, and turn-taking during conversations.

In cognitive functioning people with autism have specific strengths and specific weaknesses in the areas of perception, memory, attention, perspective-taking, and executive functioning. In the area of perception, youngsters with autism are impaired in their ability to understand others' emotional expressions. Other forms of visual perception skills, however, are intact. Although rote memory skills are strong, other types of memory seem impaired. Deficits in their ability to process meaning and categorize complex information may underlie poor performance on memory tasks. Also, limitations in language may compound memory difficulties. In the area of attention, sustained attention seems to be intact, but shifting attention is often problematic. Thus, people with autism often focus on specific aspects of the environment that might be relevant or irrelevant. Switching to other aspects is often slower and less efficient than in normally developing children. Theory of mind, the ability to understand that others have beliefs and feelings that are different from one's own, is impaired in autism.

Problems understanding these independent thoughts could explain many of the cognitive, social, and interpersonal problems in autism. In contrast to their poor performance on theory of mind tasks, persons with autism are able to show other forms of visual perspective-taking. They can describe another person's visual perspective if it does not involve understanding the other person's thoughts or feelings. Finally, many difficulties that people with autism have with planning, organization, flexibility, and impulse control could be related to deficits in controlling the internal processing of information (i.e., executive functions).

Continued research on the specific pattern of strengths and weaknesses in autism will help to show us how people with autism process information and understand their environments. We cannot assume that persons with autism are attending to what we consider the most important aspects of a task. They may have trouble planning activities, processing and remembering new information, and shifting from one task to the next. Also, they generally have a great deal of difficulty understanding our social cues. In teaching, we often guide children through our facial expressions and by explaining how our beliefs about a topic may be different from the child's. Certainly, the cognitive research suggests that these traditional approaches may not be effective. As we learn more about these cognitive variables, we will better understand how people with autism think and why they do some of the unusual things they do. Many exciting intervention ideas should be growing out of this important work in the years ahead.

5

Intervention Approaches

No aspect of autism has attracted as much interest as the subject of interventions. Autism is one of the most puzzling disorders with a generally poor prognosis for total recovery (Lockyer & Rutter, 1969). Despite this reality there have been a substantial number of alleged cures, mostly in the public media (Biklen, 1990; Maurice, 1993). One of the most difficult responsibilities of parents and professionals concerned about people with autism is to sort through the intervention literature and try to make sense out of the many conflicting claims.

   This chapter reviews the three major approaches to treatment for children with autism: psychodynamic, medical, and educational/behavioral. An effort will be made to provide an objective assessment of these approaches based on the most current empirical evidence.

PSYCHODYNAMIC

When autism was initially identified by Kanner it was generally assumed to be an emotional disorder caused by cold parents, especially mothers, who subconsciously rejected their offspring (Kanner, 1943). Because parents were viewed as the primary source of their children's autism, removal of the children from their parents' homes and their placement in residential institutions was a common recommendation made by Bettelheim, a renowned psychoanalytic practitioner, and his colleagues. "Parent-ectomies," cutting the children off from their parents, were seen as a necessary and critical component of the treatment process. Removal from their parents allowed children with autism to let down their "psychotic defenses" and begin the process of reestablishing trust with significant people in their environment. Psychodynamically oriented play therapy was an additional important component of the therapeutic process.

   Although Bettelheim claimed dramatic cures and recoveries from autism following his treatment, virtually no empirical evidence has been presented supporting the value of either removal from parents' control or traditional play therapy. In fact, the few studies that do exist show either no improvement or even deterioration. Despite the unconvincing support of these approaches others have followed with psychodynamic variations on Bettelheim.

Other psychodynamically oriented therapies have emphasized an individual therapy model rather than the removal of the child from parental control. Most of these models emphasize group therapy for the parents and individual work with the children. Child therapy strives to establish some form of positive bond between the child and therapist. Play and individual interview techniques are used and the interpretation of symbolic meanings is stressed. Some approaches attempt to reestablish relationships at earlier psychosexual stages or even to recreate early experiences like playing the sound of heartbeats to the children with autism to recreate their experience in the womb.

An example of a psychodynamically oriented approach is DesLauriers's (1978) Pheraplay. Supporting a psychodynamic interpretation of autism, Deslauriers saw the children's problems as compounded by their sensory impairments. Pheraplay was advanced as the best way to provide stimulating experiences that are intense enough to overcome autistic children's basic sensory deficits. Pheraplay differs from traditional play therapy in that the child is not taught anything specifically, but instead is encouraged to enjoy highly stimulating interpersonal interactions.

Today psychodynamically oriented approaches are infrequently used by most clinicians in the field of autism. The reasons are many, including the cumulative evidence that autism is a developmental rather than an emotional disorder, the inability of even high-functioning people with autism to conceptualize or understand underlying dynamics, and the empirical evidence demonstrating the ineffectiveness of these interventions.

Although these approaches are generally not indicated, there are still numerous instances of people with autism receiving insight-oriented therapy. The most frequent examples are the more verbal persons with autism, who are referred for their odd, nonfunctional, or inappropriate behaviors. These persons might benefit from one-to-one counseling relationships with responsible professionals, but sessions would undoubtedly be more productive if focused on concrete situations and problem solving skills rather than on insight-oriented approaches to discovering underlying psychological dynamics.

BIOLOGICAL INTERVENTIONS

Recognizing autism as a biological condition, rather than an emotional one, has led to an increased emphasis on seeking biochemical causes and a wider variety of psychopharmacological interventions. A wide range of medications currently are being used for clients with autism, depending on their related medical conditions and behavioral problems. Although pharmacological interventions have not been able to reverse the biological causes of autism to date, they can make important contributions in reducing extreme symptoms and promoting positive development. It is important, however, that these interventions be used cautiously with ongoing monitoring to ensure that they are making a contribution and that undesirable side effects are not in evidence.

Not all people with autism require, or benefit from, pharmacological interventions. In general, medications are most beneficial for clients with hyperactivity, aggressiveness, self-injurious behaviors, withdrawal, impulsive behaviors, and anxiety that significantly interferes with daily activities. Drugs should never be the sole treatment in autism but should always be part of a comprehensive and individualized overall program. Administration of medications should only be considered after a careful work-up of the patient to be sure that there are no specific allergies or other contraindications (e.g., the medication might lower the seizure threshold in a client who is prone to seizures). Pharmacological agents used in autism are anticonvulsant medications, neuroleptics, stimulants, tricyclic antidepressants, and beta-blockers, as well as lithium, clonidine, fenfluramine, naltrexone, and vitamins.

Anticonvulsant Medications

Anticonvulsant drugs are used to control seizures in autistic people in similar ways to their use with the general public. The incidence of seizures, however, is much higher in autism, so the use of these medications is more frequent (Deykin & MacMahon, 1979a). Estimates are that up to 30% of people with autism have seizures, which often develop during adolescence. Professionals working with autistic people should be especially sensitive to indications of seizures during adolescence, and those responsible for pharmacological interventions should be especially careful with any medications that might lower their seizure threshold. One anticonvulsant medication, Tegretal, has been especially effective in modifying extreme behaviors. This drug is sometimes used with aggressive clients who do not show signs of seizures.

Neuroleptics

Among the most powerful of the interventions with potentially severe side effects, neuroleptics can be helpful in modifying severe behavior problems or controlling tics in autism but should be carefully monitored and evaluated. Haldol has been the most carefully studied of this group and has been successful in reducing symptoms such as aggression, hyperactivity, and stereotypies, while increasing attention. Although dosages should be monitored individually, studies of Haldol show that it can be effective at relatively low dosages. Haldol seems most effective with older children and those with the most severe difficulties. Long-term (over 6 months) follow-up studies have demonstrated that the effects are enduring.

The major limitation of the neuroleptics is the development of tardive dyskinesia in approximately 30% of the children who take them. These dyskinesias involve involuntary movements of the face, mouth, jaw, and upper extremities. Most of these are reversible when the children are withdrawn from the medication, if they are caught quickly.

Pimozide is another neuroleptic that has received more attention recently because it is reported to be less frequently associated with tardive dyskinesia. Early studies with this medication have been promising. Another neuroleptic that has been used in autism is Mellaril. This has not had the same research support as Haldol and presents the same problem because of potential side effects. Thorazine, frequently used in schizophrenia, had some early trials with autistic people but is less favored today than the other neuroleptics because it tends to suppress all behaviors, including those considered desirable, and is likely to produce tardive dyskinesia.

Stimulants

Stimulants or amphetamines (e.g., Ritalin, Dexedrine) are sometimes helpful in reducing the hyperactivity that often accompanies autism. Although the data on these medications with autism are limited, stimulants are often prescribed to reduce hyperactivity and improve attention. Substantial evidence exists for the positive impact of these medications on behavior in students with ADD, and many believe that similar positive effects occur in autism as well. Caution should be exercised, however, because some children with autism actually deteriorate when given stimulants and others become sad and depressed. An advantage of these medications is minimal severe side effects; however, sleep problems and reduced appetites can occur.

Tricyclic Antidepressants

Clomipramine has been effective in reducing symptoms in people with OCD. Observations that some people with autism show symptoms similar to OCD have led to trials with these medications for autism. Recent studies have reported a reduction in obsessive-compulsive symptoms in clients with autism (Brasic et al., 1994; McDougle et al., 1992). Because these results are preliminary and because serious side effects, including lowering the seizure threshold, have been associated with Clomipramine, caution and close monitoring by a physician are strongly recommended.

Beta-Blockers

Although the efficacy of beta-blockers (e.g., Inderal, Tenormin) with autism has not been established, these medications have been used to decrease aggression and anxiety. Because anxiety can be so debilitating, especially in autism, and these drugs show promise even though the data are quite limited, further study is indicated.

Lithium

Lithium is typically used with bipolar disorder (manic-depressive disorders) but has more recently been tried with people with autism, especially those with cyclical patterns or very aggressive behaviors that have not responded to other forms of treatment. Lithium is especially difficult to monitor because there is a narrow range between therapeutic and toxic dosages.

Fenfluramine

Based on several observations that a neurotransmitter, serotonin, is at higher levels in people with autism than in the nonhandicapped population, the role of fenfluramine has been studied as a possible way to improve functioning in children and adults with autism. Fenfluramine, originally developed to help nonhandicapped adults lose weight, is an effective way to lower serotonin levels. A letter published in the *New England Journal of Medicine* brought this medication into the public eye with a dramatic demonstration of major IQ increases and improvements in functioning for three clients with autism. Subsequent double-blind, placebo-controlled studies have not supported the early claims and suggest that this drug might not be safe in the treatment of autistic children (Campbell, 1988).

Naltrexone

Naltrexone is a potent opiate antagonist. Its use has been based on inconclusive evidence that the behavioral problems sometimes associated with autism are possibly related to opiate abnormalities. So far, the evidence on the effectiveness of naltrexone in altering opiate levels or changing behaviors in autism has been mixed and unconvincing. There remains considerable anecdotal evidence, however, that this medication might be helpful for extreme self-injurious behaviors.

Megavitamin Therapy

Although there has been much enthusiasm over megavitamin therapy in autism, especially the combination of B6 plus magnesium, evidence for its efficacy has been mixed. Because B6 has been shown to help create enzymes needed by the brain, some experts and parents have assumed that large doses might stimulate greater brain activity. Several leaders in the field have been vocal proponents for the use of vitamins, which has stimulated considerable interest (Rimland, 1992b). At this point more research is needed, although this might represent an effective intervention under certain circumstances. Megavitamins do have side effects and so should not be administered without appropriate medical supervision.

Summary

Although pharmacological interventions are not a primary approach to treatment in autism, there has been progress over the years in finding appropriate medications to supplement treatment efforts with some children and adults with autism. A single drug or "pill" to treat autism still has not been found. Instead, several different classes of medications are used, based on the symptoms observed in specific clients. If regularly evaluated for effectiveness and possible side effects after administration, these medical interventions can make a useful contribution for some children and adults with autism on a limited basis. Intensive research on pharmacological issues continues and should offer more information in future years about the efficacy of these treatment approaches.

EDUCATIONAL/BEHAVIORAL INTERVENTIONS

A quantum leap forward in the treatment of people with autism came when behavioral techniques replaced psychotherapy as the major intervention approaches in the field. Interventions based on behavioral principles have continued to evolve and develop since those early years and remain the major interventions today. Early implementations of behavioral principles were narrowly focused on reward or punishment contingencies and their ability to increase or decrease behaviors. More recently these have expanded and diversified so that behavioral interventions can be classified according to three major groups: operant learning, cognitive, and social learning.

Operant Approaches

Operant training techniques are the straightforward applications of the basic principles of learning theory, often referred to as behavior modification. The major principles of reward and punishment are basic and easy to apply: Behaviors paired with positive events or consequences become more positive and therefore increase; those paired with negative events or consequences become more negative and therefore decrease (Skinner, 1953). The principles of positive reinforcement and punishment have been widely used with children with autism and have achieved success in improving social interaction, speech, academic skills, life skills, and a variety of other behaviors. They have also been effective in reducing inappropriate behaviors such as self-stimulation, self-injury, and aggression. Identifying appropriate reinforcers has been a major challenge because children and adults with autism do not construe or respond to their environments in the same ways as nonhandicapped people; rewards for the general population are often not rewarding for people with autism, or something that is rewarding one day loses its impact the next.

Although the principles of reward and punishment are basic and central to most operant conditioning paradigms, some modifications, adjustments, or changes in emphasis have evolved and made these approaches even more effective. The problem of finding appropriate rewards is so central to working effectively with people with autism that types and varieties of rewards have been explored above and beyond what the original operant learning theorists viewed as necessary.

Efforts also have been made to relate rewards to what is being taught, to increase their value in that context. For example, if a child learns to say the word ball during an operant conditioning language session, the boy might be given an opportunity to play outside with the "ball," rather than receiving an M&M or piece of candy as a reward. Self-reward and self-monitoring approaches have also become popular as ways of personalizing, individualizing, and hopefully increasing the salience of rewards for this population. Also, rather than trying to eliminate the unusual interests of people with autism, some programs are recognizing that these unusual interests can be effective rewards. For example, children can be rewarded with trips to bus stations or given extra time to look at maps.

The problems that children with autism have with performance, understanding, and especially communication have also led many therapists and teachers to modify their expectations. Behavioral shaping, developing successive approximations to a final goal, has become more and more common. Sophisticated techniques are now being used for breaking down complex behaviors into their simplest components to increase the opportunities for people with autism to experience success.

More recently, behavior modification approaches based on operant techniques have become increasingly popular because of the work of Lovaas (1987), one of the early pioneers in applying these techniques to children with autism in the 1960s. Although behavior modification techniques have remained a part of many treatment programs since that time, the resurgence of interest is based on Lovaas's more recent claims that intensive (30–40 or more hours per week) and very early intervention with these techniques can help these children achieve such a high level of functioning that they will be indistinguishable from normal children. Catherine Maurice's (1993) dramatic story about the "recovery" of her two children using the Lovaas approach has swept the country, exciting parents of young children with autism.

Although the Lovaas discrete trial formats, breaking down behaviors into their simplist components and constantly providing one-to-one teaching with primary contingent rewards like food, have proven effective, critics of the Lovaas approach have identified many problems with the experimental design and criteria for "recovery." They are concerned that his claims of total recovery are inflated and are raising unrealistic expectations. Arguing that autism has a biological cause, the Lovaas critics do not see how simply changing a child's behavior can alter the complex neurobiological foundations for this developmental disability. Questions about early intervention are discussed in more detail in the next chapter. For now, most would agree that operant techniques are effective, but many question the claims of "recovery" or the desirability of requiring 30–40 hours a week of vigorous one-to-one training for very young children in the home, rather than incorporating discrete trials on a more limited basis into a total school program.

Cognitive Behavioral Approaches

Cognitive approaches to learning and development have also been effective with autistic children. Based on some behavioral principles, they follow learning theory in focusing on observable behaviors rather than underlying psychodynamics. These approaches differ from operant learning behavioral techniques because they do not dismiss all unobservable variables, especially those relating to thinking, understanding, and integrating information. Although these unobservable processes are difficult to measure, they are central for cognitive theorists to understand autism.

Cognitive variables influence the way that people understand, interpret, and integrate information, the very processes that separate people with autism from the nonhandicapped population. Because understanding is so central in cognitive approaches and most of the people with autism who are studied and treated are children, developmental approaches are important to cognitive theorists. Identifying developmental levels and creating teaching strategies and approaches that match them are common strategies for cognitive theorists. Unlike many operant learning proponents, cognitive theorists acknowledge that developmental processes can differ greatly from one child to another and especially between children with autism and their nonhandicapped peers. Therefore, developmental sequences are identified separately for each child and it is not expected that normal developmental patterns will be applicable to most students with autism.

Division TEACCH (Mesibov, 1996) has been in the forefront of developing interventions for people with autism based on cognitive and developmental theory. The emphasis of TEACCH's Structured Teaching is on an autistic person's understanding of expectations and relationships in the environment. These assume greater importance than the pairing of positive consequences with desired behaviors and unpleasant consequences with undesirable behaviors. Although Structured Teaching focuses on understanding expectations and relationships, rewards and punishments are still useful, but their role is to highlight meaningful components, rather than to change behaviors by themselves through paired associate learning. Structured Teaching has five important components:

1	Organizing and simplifying the physical environment to be more consistent with the ways that people with autism process sensory information
2	Developing meaningful schedules to make each day more predictable
3	Developing individual work systems for independent functioning so that students always understand how long they will be working on tasks and when they will be finished
4	Using visually clear and meticulously organized materials and learning to identify and use visual cues so that they can facilitate generalization
5	Establishing positive and productive routines

See Table 5.1 for examples of typical Structured Teaching educational goals.

Identifying developmentally appropriate sequences and goals is accomplished through the careful use of assessment instruments. The Psychoeducational Profile-Revised (PEP-R) (Schopler, Reichler, Bashford, Lansing, & Marcus, 1990) and the Adolescent and Adult Psychoeducational Profile (AAPEP) (Mesibov, Schopler, Schaeffer, & Landrus, 1988) were created by Division TEACCH and are major components of their assessment process. These instruments are interesting and stimulating for people with autism, facilitating the engagement of these children who are often described as "untestable" when evaluated by other standardized measures. The PEP-R and AAPEP target emerging skills with which children and adults with autism have some competence, but not total mastery. These developmentally appropriate emerging skills become the focus of intervention efforts (see Table 5.2 for examples of PEP-R items and Table 5.3 for AAPEP items).

Table 5.1. Typical Structured Teaching Educational Goals for a School-Age Child[a]

1. Initiation: Student understands when it is time to make the transition or check his schedule. He stops what he is doing and goes to the transition area.
2. Identifies own schedule: Student discriminates his own schedule from others. He finds his schedule in the classroom.
3. Identifies which cue is next in sequence: Student knows which cue signifies the next activity in the sequence of the day. He takes the next cue from the left or from the top.
4. Understands meaning of visual cue: Student understands that the cues represent different locations, activities, or events. He goes to the correct location after referring to the cue.
5. Managing the schedule: Student stays on track by marking the beginning and/or end of each activity.
6. Identification of "what work": The student identifies which tasks have been assigned. This skill corresponds to the type of visual cue that labels each task basket or folder.
7. Working in an assigned sequence: The student follows an assigned sequence of tasks. This corresponds to the student's ability to identify which cue is next in the sequence of the work system, either left-to-right or top-to-bottom.
8. Completion of "how much work": The student can see exactly how many tasks have been assigned, and is able to complete these tasks within the time allotted for the work session.
9. Finding his work in the room: The student finds his assigned tasks, visually discriminating them from other tasks, activities, or objects in the room. This skill corresponds to the amount of visual stimuli he must scan in order to locate his assigned tasks.
10. Movement while working: The student brings his tasks to his desk. This skill corresponds to the distance of the tasks from his desk.
11. Staying on track/concept of "finished": The student remains focused and organized by manipulating or marking the tasks as he begins or completes each one. This skill corresponds to how he manipulates his work system, what he does with the cards, or how he checks off his assignments.
12. Movement after each task: The student places his completed tasks in the proper location. This skill corresponds to the distance of the "finished" location from his work desk.
13. Understanding "what comes next": The student accurately predicts what activity he will do after he has completed all his tasks, making the transition to the next activity. This skill corresponds to the type of visual cue used to represent "what comes next" when he is finished working.

[a]Table prepared with the assistance of Catherine Faherty from the Asheville TEACCH Center.

Social Learning Approaches

Considering the importance of the social deficit for community-based living and the overall problems of autism, surprisingly few intervention efforts have been designed to remediate social difficulties. Although many investigators acknowledge the importance of social problems in autism, inappropriate social behaviors have been hard to change and present difficult challenges for parents and professionals. One approach emphasizing the use of nonhandicapped peers to teach social behaviors shows promise. Based on work with handicapped children

Table 5.2. Sample Items from the PEP-R

1. Blows bubbles

   Materials: Jar of bubbles and blowing wand

   Administration: Demonstrate how to blow bubbles, then hand wand to child and indicate for child to blow bubbles.

   Developmental area: Fine motor

2. Taps call bell twice

   Materials: Call bell

   Administration: Put bell on table in front of child. Obtain child's attention ("Now watch what I do"). Tap bell twice in rapid succession, then indicate to child to do likewise ("You do it" or "Do exactly what I did"). If child taps bell once or several times, demonstrate again, then indicate to child to do likewise.

   Developmental area: Imitation (motor)

3. Rolls clay

   Materials: Clay or Playdough

   Administration: Divide a piece of clay between yourself and child. Demonstrate with your piece how to roll clay on table to form an elongated strand, then indicate to child to do likewise.

   Developmental area: Imitation (motor)

4. Completes geometric form board

   Scoring Note: This task is scored as two items in two developmental areas: Perception (visual) and eye–hand integration.

   Materials: 3-piece geometric form board (circle, square, triangle)

   Administration: Put geometric form board on table in front of child with base of triangle nearest child. Put circle, square, and triangle pieces, knob side up, between board and child. Make sure each piece is not opposite its own slot, then point to board and indicate to child to put in pieces. Do not point directly to any particular slot. If after a reasonable period child seems to have difficulty understanding or completing task, demonstrate with circle piece. Then return it to table and indicate to put all pieces into board.

   Developmental area: Perception (visual)

5. Expressively identifies big and little

   Materials: 3-piece size form board (mittens)

   Administration: Place largest and smallest pieces from mitten puzzle on table and remove form board. Put small piece on child's left and large piece on right. Point to pieces and say, "Look at them. They are different. In what way are they different?" Pick up large piece and ask, "Which one is this?" or "This one is . . . ?" Repeat same administration for small piece. Offer a second trial.

   Developmental area: Cognitive verbal

6. Reacts to sound of whistle

   Behavioral area: Sensory responses (auditory)

   Observational questions: Does child react inappropriately to sound of whistle, either overreacting or paying no attention at all to sound?

7. Two-way sort

   Materials: Six blocks of one color, six black checkers, and two clear plastic or glass containers

(continued)

Table 5.2. (*Continued*)

Administration: Put a block and a checker in separate containers. Demonstrate placing a second matching object in each container. Hand child other objects, one at a time, randomly alternating objects. Correct first four errors.
Developmental area: Cognitive performance

8. Catches ball
Materials: Rubber ball, 8–10" in diameter
Administration: Stand up and move away from table. Indicate to child to do likewise. Show ball to child and gesture that you are going to throw it. Stand a short distance away and gently throw ball. Note whether child catches it. Next, indicate to child to throw ball back to you. Throw ball back and forth three times.
Developmental area: Gross motor

---

without autism, the reasoning is that nonhandicapped peers could facilitate social development in their handicapped peers when brought in proximity to them and taught to model and reinforce positive social behaviors.

Strain (1984) has demonstrated the feasibility of this approach for students with autism. Strain's work is important because he recognizes that the mere presence of peers is insufficient for students with autism to learn social and communication skills. Instead, interactions and activities have to be highly structured. Strain emphasizes certain techniques that help peers work effectively with students with autism. First he helps peers understand the communicative attempts of their autistic friends so that they can learn how to respond to them immediately and enthusiastically. Through role playing peers are taught how to get their autistic friends' attention and how to initiate and maintain interactions. Specific strategies are designed for individual children based on careful assessments, including taking their hands, tapping their arms, or standing very close. Peers are also taught how to persist if a friend does not respond, how to wait for a response, and how to ignore certain inappropriate behaviors.

This preliminary work is promising and should be pursued. Clinicians and investigators should be cautioned, however, that imitation is often a severe deficit and many children with autism will have trouble benefiting from the mere presence of nonhandicapped peers. Even for more capable students with autism, the evidence is compelling that social interactions with nonhandicapped peers must be highly organized, carefully structured, and appropriately individualized for each student if these are to be beneficial. The implications of this research for educational programs is discussed in Chapter 6 on treatment issues.

A second approach to social training has been the use of social groups for people with autism. Lord and Hopkins (1986) and Mesibov (1986) have been leading these groups for the past decade, demonstrating their potential for developing social skills. Rather than the traditional focus on improving skills so

Table 5.3. Sample Items from the AAPEP

1. Sorting
   Materials: Five washers, five bolts, five standard nuts, five green buttons, sorting tray
   Administration: Place sorting tray on table in front of client with one item from each group in a compartment of its own. Place the rest of the materials in a pile in front of the client and direct client to finish sorting. If client does not begin or makes an error in sorting one of the first four items, demonstrate with one item from each group and then replace them in the pile.
2. Use of vending machines
   Materials: Two quarters, two dimes, two nickels
   Administration: Direct client to vending machine and give two quarters, two dimes, and two nickels. Indicate that client may purchase choice of items. If client does not begin or fails to complete purchase (e.g., puts in some but not enough money to buy selected item), prompt as needed in order to complete task. Closely observe client's behavior, particularly the ability to select the item desired and whether leftover change is removed from the machine.
3. Shoots baskets
   Materials: Foam rubber ball, basket
   Administration: After playing catch for a few minutes, toss the ball several times at the basket hanging on the wall. Then give the ball to client with instructions to do the same thing. If client fails to respond or begins doing something else, repeat the demonstration once and indicate to do the same. After client has performed task one time, indicate to repeat the procedure two more times.
4. Distracted by workshop sounds
   Materials: Tape recorder, cassette tape of typical workshop sounds
   Administration: After client has worked at task long enough to be able to score it, play cassette tape of typical workshop sounds and place 15 additional pencils and erasers on the table. Observe client's behavior and note whether sounds from the tape distract client from work.
5. Works without supervision
   Materials: 30 pencils, 30 slip-on erasers, empty box, stopwatch
   Administration: Administer this item when client has been working for 3 minutes or has stopped working on the previous task. Place 30 pencils and erasers on table in front of client. Indicate to client to keep working or to begin working again. While client is working, leave the room and go to observation window or far side of the room out of client's direct line of vision. Observe how long client continues to work without supervision (2 minutes maximum).
6. Works neatly and systematically
   Materials: None
   Administration: Note client's behavior while performing tasks during test session. Pay special attention to predominant mode of working.
7. Tolerates interruptions
   Materials: None
   Administration: Note client's behavior throughout the evaluation. Intentionally interrupt client when involved in a task by calling client's name and asking a question or asking client to hand you something.

that children with autism will be more normal and acceptable in society, these social groups are oriented toward making social interactions more interesting and meaningful for people with autism in order to enrich their lives. Stressing normal behaviors to people with autism who do not understand the subtleties of complex social rules and interactions can make them highly anxious and unhappy in interpersonal situations. A goal of normalcy focuses on skills and behaviors that they may never be able to fully achieve. The constant burden of expectations that they do not understand and cannot fully meet will more likely lead to withdrawal than to more involvement in social activities and interactions.

The alternative approach is to emphasize personally meaningful experiences in the company of other people. Appropriate behaviors in social situations are only emphasized to the extent that autistic people are overtly offensive or behaving in ways that violate the rights of others. Emphasis is on positive social experiences and how to enjoy the company of other people.

For example, when working with young children with autism, specific skills such as maintaining eye contact or looking at the other child are not emphasized simply because those are normal behaviors. Instead the focus is on working or playing in the proximity of other children and becoming engaged with them in activities that are interesting and meaningful. Capitalizing on this enjoyment increases and enhances social interactions.

A second example from higher functioning adults with autism might further clarify the approach. Focusing on the same principles as groups for younger children with autism, the starting point for these social programs is each member's interest and level of understanding. Many older and more verbal people with autism have idiosyncratic interests such as train stations, bus schedules, people's birthdays, or the weather. These are not necessarily inappropriate topics of conversation, but they also are not normal because they are rarely pursued by nonhandicapped people with the same intensity shown by people with autism. The intervention approach uses these interests to motivate conversations and then expands around those interests. In other words, birthdays could be a starting point for conversations with a person with autism who is very interested in them. After identifying the birthdays of all members of the group, one could then look for connections to expand the conversation. One group member might have a birthday on the same day as my cousin, so I could elaborate with more information about my cousin, where he lives, and what he likes to do during his leisure time. Expanding social interactions around the interests of people with autism is a meaningful and, consequently, effective way of increasing social interests and skills.

In order to promote social development and meaningful relationships, the participation in shared group experiences is an essential activity. The importance of shared group experiences is an underlying assumption behind the use of

Intervention Approaches   91

nonhandicapped peers as well. If autistic children share mutually satisfying and meaningful experiences with others, then they can also share in the anticipation of those activities and in the reminiscence after they are completed. In these shared group activities, the focus can be on mutual enjoyment and engagement, rather than on behaviors that others judge as normal. To the extent that group leaders observe offensive behaviors that violate others' personal rights or space, these can be addressed quickly and directly immediately after they occur.

SUMMARY

Although there is still no magical pill or cure for autism, considerable progress in treatment has occurred over the past 50 years. Early psychodynamically oriented play and group therapy techniques have been replaced by more appropriate and effective intervention strategies. Clinicians are also taking empirically validated treatment claims more seriously, so that more evidence is available today about the appropriateness and effectiveness of different treatment options.

Biological interventions have added an important component to treatment efforts. Although there is not yet any pill that cures autism, pharmacological interventions have been helpful when directed at specific symptoms and combined with other treatment approaches that develop skills and increase opportunities.

Behavioral interventions have been the most effective to date in helping people with autism. Early behavioral efforts emphasized operant conditioning techniques and have been very effective. More recently, cognitive approaches are making experiences more meaningful for people with autism, leading to better generalization and more flexibility in their skill development. Social learning theory is also becoming an effective framework for developing social skills through structured activities with nonhandicapped peers.

6

Controversial Treatment Issues

Janet lives in a group home with five other women with developmental disabilities. The women sleep two to a room, and they have round-the-clock staff supervision. Each night, one of the women helps the staff cook dinner for the group. A staff member drives the women to work at a sheltered workshop each day, where they assemble gift boxes for a mail order company.

Nathan is in the same third grade class as his normally developing twin sister. He does everything the other children do, except during reading period he works in a resource room. His teacher is trying to get a special assistant to help him while he is in the classroom. He needs more special attention than she has time to give, and an assistant could help to ease transitions and supervise his independent work.

Robert is a 3-year-old who was recently diagnosed with autism. His parents have implemented an intensive early intervention program. As part of the program, Robert works with four different trainers for a total of 40 hours a week. The trainers use a reward system to teach him words and play skills, and to reduce his stereotyped and repetitive behaviors.

Rebecca is a 4-year-old who is spending her second school year in a self-contained preschool classroom with four other students who have autism. She spends a 6-hour day in the classroom and works with a speech and language tutor twice a week. She is learning to count and identify letters. Her teachers have developed some art projects that involve skyscrapers, an area of special interest for Rebecca.

Josh is a 30-year-old man who earned a high school certificate after spending his entire school career in special education classes. For the past 5 years, he has worked in a cafeteria. He works independently, but when he began his job he had a job coach who spent the entire day with him. He lives in an apartment with another man with autism. His mother stops by once a week to make sure the men are keeping the apartment clean, eating properly, and paying the bills on time.

After having difficulty keeping any of the janitorial and food service jobs his parents found for him, Jerry moved to a rural community living center for adults with autism. Jerry spends the day tending to the animals and farming. The community members eat the food they grow. The round-the-clock staff at the center make sure that the farm work is done every day, in addition to supervising the members' self-care and leisure activities.

Previous chapters have described the short history of autism and what is known about the nature, causes, and treatment of the disability. Although specific aspects of the nature and causes of autism are still in dispute, there is general agreement among professionals about what we know and what remains to be discovered. Several general issues, however, have been especially controversial and divisive, stirring up emotional debates and arguments. The intensity of these conflicts probably reflects parental hope for a cure and professional skepticism without empirical support, as well as discrepant viewpoints in the field. Some of the more important and contentious issues of the day relate to the vignettes that introduced this chapter and include early intervention, inclusion, normalization, supported employment, punishment, labeling and specialization, and facilitated communication. Emotions surrounding these issues are often excessive; this chapter will strive for objective review with the goal of presenting the conflicting views honestly, directly, and equitably.

EARLY INTERVENTION

Early intervention is the term for services delivered to young preschool-age children with disabilities and those at risk of developing disabilities. These services are designed to lessen the long-term effects of the disability or condition. Early intervention programs are generally intensive educational efforts to stimulate development. Early intervention focusing on only the child, or the child and her family, can occur in the home, in center-based programs, or a combination of the two. Research overwhelmingly documents the importance and effectiveness of early intervention efforts (Schopler, Van Bourgondien, & Bristol, 1993) for children with autism and other developmental disabilities.

The evidence is incontrovertible that early intervention approaches are very effective at increasing developmental gains for the children and improving the functioning of their families, and result in long-term increases in skill and adaptation. Children in early intervention programs have better outcomes and need fewer special education and rehabilitation services later in their lives compared to those children who do not have these opportunities. In a recent review of eight early intervention programs, Dawson and Osterling (1997) reported that children receiving early intervention made, on average, IQ gains of approximately 20 points (see Table 6.1).

Table 6.1. Dawson and Osterling's (1997) Common Elements of Effective Early Intervention Programs

Curriculum content—an effective curriculum focuses on teaching the following skills:
1. Attention to elements of the environment
2. Imitation of others
3. Comprehension and use of language
4. Appropriate toy play
5. Appropriate social interaction

Highly supportive teaching environments and generalization strategies:
1. Low staff-to-child ratio
2. Fading the level of staff prompts as the skill is mastered

Use of predictability and routines:
1. Highly structured classrooms
2. Visual cues to help facilitate transitions between activities (e.g., object, picture, or written daily schedule)
3. Visual cues to label and define expectations during each activity (e.g., visual directions)

A functional approach to problem behaviors:
1. Focus on what the child is trying to communicate when displaying problem behaviors
2. Focus on teaching more effective communication skills
3. Allowing the children to make choices to increase their enjoyment of activities

Assistance transitioning to the elementary school classroom:
1. Teaching elementary school skills such as raising one's hand, walking in line, sitting quietly during activities, etc.
2. Helping parents to choose the most appropriate elementary school setting
3. Assistance in the training of post-preschool staff

Family involvement:
1. Education programs for parents
2. Including parents as cotherapists in their children's treatment

Although there is general agreement about the importance of early intervention in autism, questions remain about the amount, intensity, specificity, and appropriate expectations. Lovaas (1987) brought these questions to the forefront in a report on a group of 19 children with autism receiving intensive behavioral interventions (40 hours per week of one-to-one, discrete trial format training). He claims that there is a "window of opportunity" for near normal functioning with intensive intervention. Lovaas's claims, supported by a stunning personal account of one parent's successful use of this approach (Maurice, 1993), have excited parents who, in many cases, are challenging public schools to abandon what they have been doing in order to offer this intensive alternative. Considerable acrimony has been generated in the field over parents' rights to these requests and whether the Lovaas intervention with 40 hours per week of one-to-one instruction is the most effective one.

An analysis of the Lovaas technique suggests that it does produce improvements in young children with autism. There is some question, however, whether these improvements are more impressive than those resulting from a number of other intensive, structured, individualized early intervention programs (Freeman, in press). Several established early intervention programs (e.g., Division TEACCH, the Douglass Developmental Center, Pittsburgh LEEP Project) also produce substantial gains in a high percentage of children with autism. Lovaas's claims of "recovery" seem premature, given the problems reported with his nonrandom sample selection, testing procedures, and his follow-up measures, which included limited evaluations of social or communication skills (Schopler, Short, & Mesibov, 1989). What can be said is that several programs, including Lovaas's discrete trial behavior modification model, are effective and important for young children with autism and produce significant results if applied early with intensity and consistency.

Two corollaries that have grown out of the Lovaas claims are of concern to many professionals. First is the idea that more is better. Although some young children with autism might tolerate and even thrive on long hours of discrete trial format training, for many such intensive training could prove excessive and not in their best interest. Some argue that these are still young children who need more time to play, watch television, visit parks, and enjoy their free time. These professionals suggest that the number of intervention hours should be determined based on their skills, interests, attention spans, and other aspects of their behavior, level of functioning, and tolerance.

A second troubling notion for many professionals is the concept of the "window of opportunity." Believing in the existence of this window has led many parents to become frantic, worrying that if the perfect intervention is not begun before the age of 3 or 4 years then a positive outcome is impossible. Extensive research demonstrates that appropriate interventions begun after the age of 4 years can still have dramatic effects and produce high-quality outcomes for many people with autism. Parents and professionals should remember that the earlier intervention starts, the better, but it is never too late to help these children and their families.

NORMALIZATION

The normalization principle was first articulated by Wolfensberger (1972) for the American Mental Health System and has been influencing services in this country ever since. Adapted from the Scandinavian countries, it advocates for a life as close to normal as possible for people with developmental disabilities throughout the United States. When Wolfensberger first described the principle in his important and influential book, most Americans with developmental disabilities were warehoused in large and impersonal residential institutions. The impact of the principle has been to move these clients out of the institutions into smaller, more humane, community-based services.

There can be no doubt that the impact of normalization on community-based services has been profound and important. A virtual revolution has occurred in the two decades that have followed the publication of the Wolfensberger book, and people with handicaps are now more integrated and meaningfully involved in their communities with an increasing range of residential and vocational options. The impact of these changes has been dramatic and very positive. Unfortunately and ironically, the concept of normalization that initially led to more diversity and better services is now blocking growth and possibilities by limiting potential options. Certainly community-based facilities are an important advance, but people with handicaps, especially when they are as severe as autism, still need a multitude of services and should be allowed to pursue options best suited to their needs.

The problem that has evolved is that services appearing unusual or not normal are being summarily dismissed as inappropriate. We have, therefore, moved from saying that we need more diversity and better community-based services to arguing that no one should live in residential institutions or any facilities resembling them because these programs are not normal. This is an unfortunate development, as those with autism are extremely diverse and virtually any service we can imagine will probably be the most appropriate one for a subgroup of people with autism. To summarily dismiss these options and deny them to people with autism can be as limiting and inappropriate as was warehousing all developmentally handicapped people two decades ago.

An example of this problem is the opposition of many normalization followers to the development of rural, agriculture-based small communities.

Somerset Court in England was a pioneer of this model that has been followed in the United States by two superb prototypes, Bittersweet Farms and the Carolina Living and Learning Center (CLLC). These programs have identified two problems that are frequently faced by people with autism in community-based services: overstimulation and lack of coordinated programming. Agriculturally based rural environments are quieter and calmer than cities and are better suited to people with autism who experience extreme anxiety and agitation in response to environmental stimulation. These programs also coordinate all aspects of their clients' lives: Their clients plant the seeds, harvest the crops, eat the resulting food, and then clean up the leftovers. The predictable and consistent daily rhythm of these programs can be very reassuring for a subgroup of people with autism who have difficulty with any changes or unexpected disruptions.

This discussion of the normalization principle is in no way designed to minimize its impact or importance. Instead it is meant to highlight the need for a variety of services and to point out the potential danger when advocates for new approaches also argue for eliminating everything that came before. There are enough unique needs and different kinds of people with autism that any reasonable and well-thought-out change will bring about a response in some of them. Our field will be better served if advocates expend their energy on supporting their own new ideas, rather than on eliminating other approaches.

INCLUSION

"Full inclusion" is based on the assumption that students with disabilities should be involved in regular education. It has evolved from the practices of integration and mainstreaming. The essence of full inclusion is that students with special needs should be educated with typical students in regular classes with appropriate support services, rather than be placed in resource rooms, special education classrooms, or special schools. Full inclusion goes beyond mainstreaming; in mainstreaming students have a special education setting as their home base, while full inclusion endorses the regular classroom as the home base for all students with or without disabilities. Advocates contend that the benefits of full inclusion include increased expectations by teachers, behavioral modeling by normally developing peers, greater learning, higher self-esteem, more accepting attitudes by peers, and less isolation and stigma for students with disabilities and their families.

As we too often see in education, the movement for full inclusion has dismissed the "continuum of services" concept before generating adequate systematic research on inclusion's effectiveness. In fact a recent review of the literature suggests much stronger support for a continuum of services than a full inclusion model for students with autism (Mesibov & Shea, 1996). Inclusion's advocates argue that the issue is one of human rights rather than of education. Unfortunately for many students with autism, indiscriminately enforcing their right to participate in regular educational settings sometimes compromises their need for specialized and individualized services.

Over the past 15 years there have been five significant literature reviews or meta-analyses on special class versus regular class placements for students with disabilities (see Mesibov & Shea, 1996). These reviews are not uniformly supportive of fully included placements. What they show are slight trends favoring integrated over segregated programs. There is, however, considerable variability among the findings and indications that some students benefit more from segregated classrooms or programs, especially students with more severe handicaps, learning problems, and behavioral difficulties.

Although the literature on full inclusion and autism is more limited, it suggests the same conclusions. Many people with autism have limited communication skills, unusual sensory processing mechanisms, difficulty integrating ideas, confusion when interpreting meaning and relationships, and problems with unpredictability and change. Many of them need specialized instruction in specifically designed settings to minimize these deficits and help them to learn effective coping and integration strategies. Traditional educational techniques, appropriate for other students, are often ineffective for this group. Students with autism fare better through structured teaching approaches that emphasize visual presentations of materials, highlight relevant concepts, and minimize sensory distractions. These approaches have proven most effective and are often more easily implemented in specialized educational settings (Mesibov, Schopler, & Hearsey, 1994). There are, however, some higher-functioning people with autism who do very well in regular education settings if these structured teaching ideas are used as support.

Starting their education with a strong self-contained component makes the most sense for many students with autism. Although most students with autism can learn to function effectively in more integrated settings, the process should be gradual, especially for those who are agitated or overstimulated by sensory input. As their learning and coping skills develop they can gradually and more effectively be integrated into more normal educational settings and environments.

SUPPORTED EMPLOYMENT

Philosophies similar to those underlying inclusion have also influenced vocational work settings for adults with disabilities. The reasoning is that if children with disabilities can function in school programs with minimal support, then adults with disabilities should be able to work productively in vocational settings.

Supported employment is defined as individuals with disabilities working in regular job or business settings for a minimum of 20 hours per week. These workers receive wages and benefits similar to those offered to nonhandicapped employees, but they have regular support services available to help them learn the jobs and maintain their effectiveness and productivity. Four models of supported employment have been described and implemented with people with autism: job coach model, enclave, small business model, and mobile crew.

The job coach model has a trainer working directly with the individual client with autism. The job coach locates the job, learns how to do it, and breaks it down into smaller tasks for the client with autism. The job coach then goes on site with the client for up to 2 months to teach the client the job and train the coworkers about autism and any special needs or peculiarities they might encounter. After 8–10 weeks, the job coach gradually decreases her participation on site, but maintains regular follow-up contact by telephone or site visits.

Enclaves include a group of up to eight people with disabilities and at least one full-time job coach working in a business or industry. Individuals in an enclave are paid directly by the business or industry for which they work. Enclave clients are typically disbursed throughout the setting and the job coach rotates among them, providing help and support as needed. Enclaves are especially good for clients with excellent work skills who cannot function totally independently in vocational settings.

Maintaining a business in a community where five to ten individuals with autism are employed along with an equal, or greater, number of nonhandicapped clients is the small business model. The particular business is one that emphasizes the strengths of the clients with autism, such as baking, printing, or electronics. The small business model allows a maximum of supervision and assistance for the clients with autism because the owners have established the business with their needs in mind.

Mobile crews are small groups of disabled workers and a supervisor who complete service jobs at various locations in a community. The mobile crew leader locates jobs and supervises the workers on those jobs. Most mobile crews are involved in house cleaning, yard work, or janitorial work. Clients who need more supervision than the other supported employment models allow are often placed in these programs.

Supported employment is an exciting new possibility for disabled people in employment settings. It can be viewed as an additional option for clients who previously were limited to working in workshops for people with disabilities. In their enthusiasm for supported employment, however, some advocates have suggested that all handicapped workshops should be dismantled and replaced by supported employment programs. Dismantling all workshops would not be in the best interest of people with autism who require a wide range of services in a variety of different settings. Sheltered workshops can be an important component of a continuum of services for people with autism, allowing more flexibility for clients who need extensive accommodations in their schedules, routines, physical environments, or daily activities. People with autism are better served when supported employment is an option that supplements existing sheltered workshop settings, rather than replacing them.

PUNISHMENT

Questions concerning punishment or aversive procedures have been very controversial in the field of autism. Most parents and professionals are uncomfortable using negative consequences to decrease inappropriate behaviors because these strategies feel inhumane to them. On the other hand, some of the extreme and dangerous behaviors exhibited by people with autism, such as self-injurious behaviors, require extraordinary intervention measures. Those who support continuous use of aversives with stringent safeguards point out their effectiveness in controlling extreme behavior problems.

One reason for the disagreement over the use of punishment is that two related aspects are often confused. One question is whether or not mild punishment or aversive negative consequences should be part of ongoing behavior modification programs. The second question is whether more powerful aversive procedures should be condoned under any circumstances, even when dealing with life-threatening behaviors.

The first question about changing frequent inappropriate behaviors by negative behavior modification procedures has been, for the most part, resolved. Early proponents of behavioral techniques argued that there must be a marked contrast between positive reinforcers that increase desirable behaviors and negative consequences that decrease undesirable behaviors in order for these techniques to be powerful and effective for handicapped people. More recently, several investigators (LaVigna & Donnellan, 1986; Mesibov et al., 1994) have demonstrated that positive reinforcement techniques, when applied systematically and intensively, are powerful enough to control and develop appropriate behaviors without a need for aversive procedures. Today most autism professionals support the use of positive reinforcement techniques and emphasize these positive approaches with their clients.

Opinions about the use of aversive procedures for severe and even life-threatening behaviors are more divided. Arguments against aversives are based on a distaste for these intervention strategies and a commitment to the rights of citizens with autism to humane treatment options. These debates can become quite emotional. Opponents of aversive interventions argue that experimental data supports the use of positive interventions and suggests that these approaches are effective with all behaviors. They view aversive interventions as inappropriate and unnecessary.

LaVigna and Donnellan (1986) have advanced the position that aversive procedures are unnecessary and only nonaversive interventions should be practiced in the field of autism. They argued that differential reinforcements of alternative behaviors, stimulus change and control procedures, and various respondent conditioning approaches are adequate to eliminate undesirable negative behaviors and promote more positive alternatives.

Proponents of maintaining the option to use aversive procedures under strict guidelines argue that the right to appropriate treatment is the highest priority. They maintain that the evidence favoring nonaversive approaches, especially for more severe behavioral difficulties of more severely handicapped clients, is sparse and unconvincing. An impartial consensus panel convened by the National Institutes of Health (1990) supported this position, concluding that interventions for extreme behaviors must be complex and multifaceted, including many different approaches. Presently, aversive procedures are still permitted for extreme behavior problems like life-threatening self-injury under carefully controlled conditions. The situation will be closely monitored by advocates on both sides of the issue.

LABELING AND SPECIALIZATION

The question of whether or not to label young children according to current diagnostic categories has created controversy over the years. Opponents of labels argue that they can be inaccurate, especially with young children; are often stigmatizing; and can create problems above and beyond the handicaps. They also propose that labels have little impact on instructional programs, which should be based on careful assessments of individual needs, not on generic solutions associated with particular labels.

Although the arguments against labeling have merit and labels have contributed to some unfortunate situations, there are important benefits to labeling that outweigh these difficulties. Labels, though perhaps not always as productive and helpful as we might like, do serve important functions: Labels are helpful for parents, they guide resource identification and dissemination, and they help identify specialized aspects of unique conditions such as autism.

Parents, sometimes resistant to labeling their children, prefer having a name for their child's differences in the long run. Many parents of older children report their struggles with the labeling process, but reiterate the importance of a label, even if it is not the one they prefer or would choose (Akerley, 1984). Even worse than a label, according to many parents, is to know that something is different about their child and yet not know what it is called or what to expect. Most parents will continue their search until someone can offer them a specific name for their child's condition. Even though some labels like "autism" are difficult to accept, most parents assert that the label is preferable to not knowing a name for their child's condition.

Naming a child's disability is helpful for a parent's peace of mind, and it also guides their search for information and identifies professional services that might be useful. Without labels, there is not any way of locating research or others struggling with similar challenges. These advantages of labels are also important for professionals assisting parents. Appropriate labels provide access to the larger community working with children having similar needs.

Finally, labels are especially important in the field of autism because specialized approaches have been developed that are effective with these youngsters. In order to benefit from these approaches, a child must be identified so that parents and professionals can be educated about these children's problems with change, conceptualization, play, communication, and social relationships. Innovative teaching strategies and specialized approaches to organizing learning and living environments have resulted in dramatic progress for these children over the past decade; however, they must be identified first to reap the benefits. Appropriate identification is essential for these children to receive the services they require and for professionals and parents to receive appropriate training and support to implement effective treatment programs.

FACILITATED COMMUNICATION

Facilitated communication (FC), a form of assisted communication, was first introduced into the United States by Biklen (1990). Promoted as a dramatic new strategy for severely and profoundly retarded people with autism, FC was said to reveal untapped literacy and complex emotional expression in people with autism. FC was adapted from Rosemary Crossley's work in Australia and involves supporting the arm of a person with autism during communication with a computer or comparable keyboard configuration. Supporters report amazing success with this intervention; some claim up to 90% of people previously thought to be nonverbal were able to communicate through FC.

Proponents of FC are proposing a reconceptualization of autism. Rather than accepting the conventional wisdom that 70% of this group also have mental retardation, they are suggesting that FC reveals at least average intelligence and great sensitivity in virtually all people with autism (Rimland, 1992a). Fascinated by these possibilities many investigators have been studying the basic paradigm. Much of the attention has been focused on clarifying the influence of the facilitator in the message. Perhaps the facilitator is inadvertently influencing the message by guiding the arm of the client? Shane (1994) reports the results of these studies, which overwhelmingly refute the claims for FC. Once controlled conditions are imposed, the evidence for hidden literacy or complex emotional expression disappears. Of over 300 clients studied in the literature virtually none have been able to demonstrate complex communication skills without facilitator influence.

The FC experience reminds us how important it is to test one's theories carefully and thoroughly. Parents of handicapped people are a vulnerable group, especially when there is the promise of dramatic progress. Before proposing new ideas or techniques that might tap into this vulnerability it is crucial for professionals to test them fully, skeptically, and comprehensively.

SUMMARY

Autism is a difficult disability for parents and professionals to understand and cope with. It is not surprising that some issues in the field arouse strong emotions and controversy. Because no one approach or intervention has proven totally successful, disagreements about appropriate interventions frequently arise. Recent controversies have developed around early intervention, inclusion, supported employment, the use of aversives, and labeling. Presently, there are no cures for autism and nothing that helps everyone. On the other hand, progress is being made and certain models or approaches are having an impact on individual clients and their families. Perhaps the best way to foster progress at this point is for parents and professionals to put their time and energy into honestly promoting their own work rather than expending their considerable energy criticizing others.

Epilogue

It has been more than 50 years since Leo Kanner wrote the initial paper describing autism. In the early years immediately following his publication, progress was slow because the then popular psychodynamic model put the focus on the parents, rather than the children. As the biological determinants of autism became better understood and more widely accepted in the 1970s and 1980s, progress has accelerated dramatically. Our current understanding of autism is much better and increases daily. Prospects for the future seem bright.

Today we understand autism as a neurobiological condition that affects how people perceive and understand the world. The diagnosis of autism is becoming more systematic and is possible at much younger ages. Although we have not identified the precise mode of genetic transmission, we do know that there is a strong genetic component in many cases, and other causes of autism have been identified as well. It is feasible that we will soon be able to identify the specific cause in many individual cases.

Progress is being made in understanding the neurological sequelae to autism. Theories about the parts of the brain that are most affected are still speculative, but our understanding is growing and resulting in increasingly effective biological treatments. Social and communication deficits are better understood and more effectively remediated. Early intervention holds the promise for enduring gains.

As we approach the twenty-first century, the problem of autism is far from solved. On the other hand, there is every reason to be optimistic when we think about the amazing progress that we have made in our short history and the marked improvements we have observed in the quality of life of these people and their families. The next decade should see exciting new developments in our understanding of this disability and more effective ways to help these people and their families.

References

American Psychiatric Association. (1980). *Diagnostic and statistical manual* (3rd ed.). Washington, DC: Author.

American Psychiatric Association. (1987). *Diagnostic and statistical manual* (3rd ed. rev.). Washington, DC: Author.

American Psychiatric Association. (1994). *Diagnostic and statistical manual* (4th ed.). Washington, DC: Author.

Arkerley, M. S. (1984). Developmental changes in families with autistic children: A parent's perspective. In E. Schopler & G. B. Mesibov (Eds.), *The effects of autism on the family* (pp. 85–98). New York: Plenum.

Asperger, H. (1979). Problems of infantile autism. *Communication, 13*, 45–52.

Asperger, H. (1991). "Autistic Psychopathy" in childhood. In U. Frith (Ed. & Trans.), *Autism and Asperger syndrome* (pp. 37–92). Cambridge, England: Cambridge University Press. (Original work published 1944).

Bachevalier, J. (1994). Medial temporal lobe structures and autism: A review of clinical and experimental findings. *Neuropsychologia, 32*, 627–648.

Bachevalier, J. (1996). Brief report: Medial temporal lobe in autism: A putative animal model in primates. *Journal of Autism and Developmental Disorders, 26*, 217–220.

Bailey, A., Bolton, P., Butler, L., Le Couteur, A., Murphy, M., Scott, S., Webb, T., & Rutter, M. (1993). Prevalence of the fragile X anomaly amongst autistic twins and singletons. *Journal of Child Psychology and Psychiatry, 34*, 673–688.

Bailey, A., Le Couteur, A., Gottesman, I., Bolton, P., Simonoff, E., Yuzda, E., & Rutter, M. (1995). Autism as a stongly genetic disorder: Evidence from a British twin study. *Psychological Medicine, 25*, 63–78.

Bailey, A., Phillips, W., & Rutter, M. (1996). Autism: Toward an integration of clinical, genetic, neuropsychological and neurobiological perspectives. *Journal of Child Psychology and Psychiatry, 27*, 89–126.

Baird, G., Baron-Cohen, S., Bohman, M., Coleman, M., Frith, U., Gillberg, C., Gillberg, C., Howlin, P., Mesibov, G., Peeters, T., Ritvo, E., Steffenburg, S., Taylor, D., Waterhouse, L., Wing, L., & Zapella, M. (1991). Autism is not necessarily a Pervasive Developmental Disorder [Letter to the editor]. *Developmental Medicine and Child Neurology, 33*, 363–364.

Baron-Cohen, S., Cox, A., Baird, G., Swettenham, J., Nightingale, N., Morgan, K., Drew, A., & Charman, T. (1996). Psychological markers in the detection of autism in infancy in a large population. *British Journal of Psychiatry, 168*, 158–163.

Baron-Cohen, S., Leslie, A. M., & Frith, U. (1985). Does the autistic child have a "theory of mind"? *Cognition, 21*, 37–46.

Bauman, M., & Kemper, T. (1985). Limbic and cerebellar abnormalitites: Consistent findings in infantile autism. *Journal of Neuropathology and Experimental Neurology, 47*, 369.

Bettelheim, B. (1967). *The empty fortress.* New York: The Free Press.

Biklen, D. (1990). Communication unbound: Autism and praxis. *Harvard Educational Review, 60,* 291–314.

Biklen, D. (1992). Facilitated communication: Biklen responds. *American Journal of Speech-Language Pathology, 1,* 18–20.

Bleuler, E. (1950). *Dementia praecox or the group of schizophrenias.* New York: International Universities Press. (Original work published 1911).

Bolton, P., Macdonald, H., Pickles, A., Rios, P., Goode, S., Crowson, M., Bailey, A., & Rutter, M. (1994). A case-control family history study of autism. *Journal of Child Psychology and Psychiatry, 35,* 877–900.

Bolton, P., & Rutter, M. (1990). Genetic influences in autism. *International Review of Psychiatry, 2,* 67–80.

Boucher, J. (1977). Hand preference in autistic children and their parents. *Journal of Autism and Childhood Schizophrenia, 7,* 177–187.

Boucher, J. (1981a). Immediate free recall in early childhood autism: Another point of behavioral similarity with amnesic syndrome. *British Journal of Psychology, 72,* 211–215.

Boucher, J. (1981b). Memory for recent events in autistic children. *Journal of Autism and Developmental Disorders, 11,* 293–301.

Boucher, J., & Lewis, V. (1989). Memory impairments and communication in relatively able autistic children. *Journal of Child Psychology and Psychiatry, 30,* 99–122.

Boucher, J., & Warrington, E. (1976). Memory deficits in early infantile autism: Some similarities to the amnesic syndrome. *British Journal of Psychology, 67,* 73–87.

Brasic, J. R., Barnett, J. Y., Kaplan, D., & Sheitman, B. B. (1994). Clomipramine ameliorates adventitious movements and compulsions in prepubertal boys with autistic disorder and severe mental retardation. *Neurology, 44,* 1309–1312.

Campbell, M. (1988). Fenfluramine treatment of autism. *Journal of Child Psychology and Psychiatry and Allied Disciplines, 29,* 1–10.

Campbell, M., Anderson, L. T., Small, A. M., Adams, P., Gonzalez, N. W., & Ernst, M. (1993). Naltrexone in autistic children: Behavioral symptoms and attentional learning. *Journal of the American Academy of Child and Adolescent Psychiatry, 32,* 1283–1291.

Campbell, M., Geller, B., Small, A. M., Petti, T. A., & Ferris, S. H. (1978). Minor physical anomalies in young psychotic children. *American Journal of Psychiatry, 135,* 573–575.

Cantwell, D. P., Baker, L., & Rutter, M. (1979). Families of autistic and dysphasic children. *Archives of General Psychiatry, 36,* 682–687.

Carson, R. C., & Sanislow, C. A. (1993). The schizophrenias. In P. B. Sutker & H. E. Adams (Eds.), *Comprehensive handbook of psychopathology* (pp. 295–333). New York: Plenum.

Chance, P. (1974). "After you hit a child, you can't just get up and leave him; you are hooked to that kid": A conversation with Ivar Lovaas about self-mutilating children and how their parents make it worse. *Psychology Today, 7,* 76–84.

Chess, S. (1971). Autism in children with congenital rubella. *Journal of Autism and Childhood Schizophrenia, 1,* 33–47.

Chess, S. (1977). Follow-up report on autism in congenital rubella. *Journal of Autism and Childhood Schizophrenia, 7,* 69–81.

Ciaranello, A. L., & Ciaranello, R. D. (1995). The neurobiology of infantile autism. *Annual Review of Neuroscience, 18,* 101–128.

Ciaranello, R. D. (1995, March/April). An interview with Roland Ciaranello, M.D. *The Advocate,* 14–15.

Cohen, D. J., Caparulo, B. K., Shaywitz, B. A., & Bowers, M. B. (1977). Dopamine and serotonin metabolism in neuropsychiatrically disturbed children. *Archives of General Psychiatry, 34,* 545–550.

Colbert, E. G., Koegler, R. R., & Markham, C. H. (1959). Vestibular dysfunction in childhood schizophrenia. *Archives of General Psychiatry, 1,* 600–617.

Colby, K. M., & Parkison, C. (1977). Handedness in autistic children. *Journal of Autism and Childhood Schizophrenia, 7,* 3–9.

Courchesne, E., Press, G. A., & Yeung-Courchesne, R. (1993). Parietal lobe abnormalities detected with magnetic resonance in patients with infantile autism. *American Journal of Roentgenology, 160,* 387–393.

Courchesne, E., Townsend, J. P., Akshoomoff, N. A., Yeung-Courchesne, R., Press, G. A., Murakami, J. W., Lincoln, A. J., James, H. E., Saitoh, O., Egaas, B., Haas, R. H., & Schreibman, L. (1994). A new finding: Impairment in shifting attention in autistic and cerebellar patients. In H. Broman & J. Grafman (Eds.), *Atypical cognitive deficits in developmental disorders: Implications for brain function* (pp. 101–137). Hillsdale, NJ: Erlbaum.

Courchesne, E., Yeung-Courchesne, R., Press, G. A., Hesselink, J. R., & Jernigan, T. L. (1988). Hypoplasia of cerebellar vermal lobules VI and VII in autism. *New England Journal of Medicine, 318,* 1349–1354.

Cox, R. D., & Mesibov, G. B. (1995). Relationship between autism and learning disabilities. In E. Schopler & G. B. Mesibov (Eds.), *Learning and cognition in autism* (pp. 57–70). New York: Plenum.

Dawson, G. (1996). Brief report: Neuropsychology of autism: A report on the state of the science. *Journal of Autism and Developmental Disorders, 26,* 179–184.

Dawson, G., & Adams, A. (1984). Imitation and social responsiveness in autistic children. *Journal of Abnormal Child Psychology, 12,* 209–225.

Dawson, G., Finley, C., Phillips, S., & Galpert, L. (1986). Hemispheric specialization and the language abilities of autistic children. *Child Development, 57,* 1440–1453.

Dawson, G., Klinger, L. G., Panagiotides, H., Lewy, A., & Castelloe, P. (1995). Subgroups of autistic children based on social behavior display distinct patterns of brain activity. *Journal of Abnormal Child Psychology, 23,* 569–583.

Dawson, G., & Lewy, A. (1989a). Arousal, attention, and the socioemotional impairments of individuals with autism. In G. Dawson (Ed.), *Autism: Nature, diagnosis and treatment* (pp. 49–74). New York: Guilford.

Dawson, G., & Lewy, A. (1989b). Reciprocal subcortical-cortical influences in autism: The role of attentional mechanisms. In G. Dawson (Ed.), *Autism: Nature, diagnosis, and treatment* (pp. 144–173). New York: Guilford.

Dawson, G., & Osterling, J. (1997). Early intervention in autism. In M. J. Guralnick (Ed.), *The effectiveness of early intervention* (pp. 307–326). Baltimore: Paul Brookes.

Dawson, G., Warrenburg, S., & Fuller, P. (1983). Hemisphere functioning and motor imitation in autistic persons. *Brain and Cognition, 2,* 346–354.

DesLauriers, A. M. (1978). Play, symbols, and the development of language. In M. Rutter & E. Schopler (Eds.), *Autism: A reappraisal of concepts and treatment* (pp. 313–326). New York: Plenum.

Despert, J. L. (1951). Some considerations relating to the genesis of autistic behavior in children. *American Journal of Orthopsychiatry, 21,* 335–350.

Deykin, E. Y., & MacMahon, G. (1979a). The incidence of seizures among children with autism. *American Journal of Psychiatry, 136,* 1310–1312.

Deykin, E. Y., & MacMahon, G. (1979b). Viral exposure and autism. *American Journal of Epidemiology, 109,* 628–638.

DiLavore, P. C., Lord, C., & Rutter, M. (1995). The pre-linguistic diagnostic observation schedule. *Journal of Autism and Developmental Disorders, 25,* 355–379.

du Verglas, G., Banks, S. R., & Guyer, K. E. (1988). Clinical effects of fenfluramine on children with autism: A review of the research. *Journal of Autism and Developmental Disorders, 18,* 297–308.

Dykens, E., Leckman, J. F., Paul, R., & Watson, M. (1988). Cognitive, behavioral, and adaptive functioning in fragile X and non-fragile X retarded men. *Journal of Autism and Developmental Disorders, 18,* 41–52.

Eisenberg, L., & Kanner, L. (1956). Early infantile autism 1943–1955. *American Journal of Orthopsychiatry, 26,* 556–566.

Elia, M., Musumeci, S. A., & Ferri, R. (1995). Clinical and neurophysiological aspects of epilepsy in subjects with autism and mental retardation. *American Journal on Mental Retardation, 100,* 6–16.

Ferster, C. B. (1961). Positive reinforcement and behavioral deficits of autistic children. *Child Development, 32,* 437–456.

Ferster, C. B., & DeMyer, M. K. (1961). The development of performances in autistic children in an automatically controlled environment. *Journal of Chronic Diseases, 13,* 312–345.

Folstein, S., & Rutter, M. (1977). Infantile autism: A genetic study of 21 twin pairs. *Journal of Child Psychology and Psychiatry, 18,* 297–321.

Freeman, B. J. Guidelines for evaluating programs for autistic children. *Journal of Autism and Developmental Disorders* (in press).

Frith, U. (1989). *Autism: Explaining the enigma.* Oxford, England: Blackwell.

Frith, U., & Hermelin, B. (1969). The role of visual and motor cues for normal, subnormal and autistic children. *Journal of Child Psychology and Psychiatry, 10,* 153–163.

Gersten, R. M. (1980). In search of the cognitive deficit in autism: Beyond the stimulus overselectivity model. *The Journal of Special Education, 14,* 47–65.

Gillberg, C. (1984). Infantile autism and other childhood psychoses in a Swedish urban region: Epidemiological aspects. *Journal of Child Psychology and Psychiatry, 25,* 35–43.

Gillberg, C., & Coleman, M. (1992). *The biology of the autistic syndromes* (2nd ed.), London: Mac Keith.

Gillberg, C., Steffenburg, S., & Schaumann, H. (1991). Is autism more common now than ten years ago? *British Journal of Psychiatry, 158,* 403–409.

Gillberg, C., Steffenburg, S., Wahlstrom, J., Gillberg, I. C., Sjostedt, A., Martinsson, T., Liedgren, S., & Eeeg-Olofsson, O. (1991). Autism associated with marker chromosome. *Journal of the American Academy of Child and Adolescent Psychiatry, 30,* 489–494.

Gordon, N. (1990). Acquired aphasia in childhood: The Landau–Kleffner syndrome. *Developmental Medicine and Child Neurology, 32,* 270–274.

Grandin, T., & Scariano, M. M. (1986). *Emergence labeled autistic.* Novato, California: Arena Press.

Happé, F., & Frith, U. (1991). Is autism a Pervasive Developmental Disorder? Debate and argument: How useful is the "PDD" label? *Journal of Child Psychology and Psychiatry, 32,* 1167–1168.

Hashimoto, T., Tayama, M., Murakawa, K., & Yoshimoto, T. (1995). Development of the brainstem and cerebellum in autistic patients. *Journal of Autism and Dvelopmental Disorders, 25,* 1–18.

Heh, C. W., Smith, R., Wu, J., Hazlett, E., Russell, A., Asarnow, R., Tanguay, P., & Buchsbaum, M. S. (1989). Positron emission tomography of the cerebellum in autism. *American Journal of Psychiatry, 146,* 242–245.

Hertzig, M. E., Snow, M. E., New, E., & Shapiro, T. (1990). DSM-III and DSM-III-R diagnosis of autism and Pervasive Developmental Disorders in nursery school children. *Journal of the American Academy of Child and Adolescent Psychiatry, 29,* 123–126.

Hobson, P. (1992). Social perception in autism. In E. Schopler & G. B. Mesibov (Eds.), *High-functioning individuals with autism* (pp. 157–184). New York: Plenum.

Hobson, R. P. (1984). Early childhood autism and the question of egocentrism. *Journal of Autism and Developmental Disorders, 14,* 85–104.

Hobson, R. P. (1996). *Autism and the development of mind.* Hillsdale, NJ: Erlbaum.

Hsu, M., Yeung-Courchesne, R., Courchesne, E., & Press, G. A. (1991). Absence of magnetic resonance imaging evidence of pontine abnormality in infantile autism. *Archives of Neurology, 48,* 1160–1163.

Hunt, A., & Shepherd, C. (1993). A prevalence study of autism in tuberous sclerosis. *Journal of Autism and Developmental Disorders, 23,* 323–339.

Kanner, L. (1943). Autistic disturbances of affective contact. *Nervous Child, 2,* 217–250.

Kanner, L. (1949). Problems of nosology and psychodynamics in early infantile autism. *American Journal of Orthopsychiatry, 19,* 416–426.

Kerbeshian, J., Burd, L., & Fisher, W. (1990). Asperger's syndrome: To be or not to be? *British Journal of Psychiatry, 156,* 721–725.

Kleiman, M. D., Neff, S., & Rosman, N. P. (1992). The brain in infantile autism: Are posterior fossa structures abnormal? *Neurology, 42,* 753–760.

Klinger, L. G., & Dawson, G. (1995). A fresh look at categorization abilities in persons with autism. In E. Schopler & G. Mesibov (Eds.), *Learning and cognition in autism* (pp. 119–136). New York: Plenum.

Kurita, H. (1985). Infantile autism with speech loss before the age of thirty months. *Journal of the American Academy of Child Psychiatry, 24,* 191–196.

LaVigna, G. W., & Donnellan, A. (1986). *Alternatives to punishment: Solving behavior problems with non-aversive strategies.* New York: Irvington.

Le Couteur, A., Bailey, A., Goode, S., Robertson, S., Gottesman, I., Schmidt, D., & Rutter, M. (1996). A broader phenotype of autism: The clinical spectrum in twins. *Journal of Child Psychology and Psychiatry 37,* 785–801.

Lee, A., Hobson, R. P., & Chiat, S. (1994). I, you, me, and autism: An experimental study. *Journal of Autism and Developmental Disorders, 24,* 155–176.

Lincoln, A. J., Allen, M. H., & Kilman, A. (1992). The assessment and interpretation of intellectual abilities in people with autism. In E. Schopler and G. B. Mesibov (Eds.), *Learning and cognition in autism* (pp. 89–117). New York: Plenum.

Lobascher, M. E., Kingerlee, P. E., & Gubbay, S. S. (1970). Childhood autism: An investigation of aetiological factors in twenty-five cases. *British Journal of Psychiatry, 117,* 525–529.

Lockyer, L., & Rutter, M. (1969). A five to fifteen year follow-up study of infantile psychosis. III. Psychological aspects. *British Journal of Psychiatry, 115,* 865–882.

Lord, C., & Hopkins, J. M. (1986). The social behaviour of autistic children with younger and same-age nonhandicapped peers. *Journal of Autism and Developmental Disorders, 16,* 249–262.

Lord, C., Mulloy, C., Wendelboe, M., & Schopler, E. (1991). Pre- and perinatal factors in high-functioning females and males with autism. *Journal of Autism and Developmental Disorders, 21,* 197–209.

Lord, C., Rutter, M., Goode, S., Heemsbergen, J., Jordan, H., Mawhood, L., & Schopler, E. (1989). Autism diagnostic observation schedule: A standardized observation of communicative and social behavior. *Journal of Autism and Developmental Disorders, 19,* 185–212.

Lord, C., Rutter, M., & Le Couteur, A. (1994). Autism diagnostic interview-revised: A revised version of a diagnostic interview for caregivers of individuals with possible pervasive developmental disorders. *Journal of Autism and Developmental Disorders, 24,* 659–685.

Lord, C., & Schopler, E. (1987). Neurobiological implications of sex differences in autism. In E. Schopler & G. B. Mesibov (Eds.), *Neurobiological issues in autism* (pp. 191–211). New York: Plenum.

Lovaas, O. I. (1987). Behavioral treatment and normal educational and intellectual functioning in young autistic children. *Journal of Consulting and Clinical Psychology, 55,* 3–9.

Lovaas, O. I., Berberich, J. P., Perloff, B. F., & Shaeffer, B. (1966). Acquisition of imitative speech by schizophrenic children. *Science, 151,* 705–707.

Lovaas, O. I., Freitag, G., Gold, V. J., & Kassorla, I. C. (1965). Experimental studies in childhood schizophrenia: Analysis of self-destructive behavior. *Journal of Experimental Child Psychology, 2,* 67–84.

Lovaas, O. I., Koegel, R. L., & Schreibman, L. (1979). Stimulus overselectivity in autism: A review of research. *Psychological Bulletin, 86,* 1236–1254.

Lovaas, O. I., Schreibman, L., & Koegel, R. L. (1974). A behavior modification approach to the treatment of autistic children. *Journal of Autism and Childhood Schizophrenia, 4,* 111–129.

Loveland, K. A., Tunali-Kotoski, B., Pearson, D. A., Brelsford, K. A., Ortegon, J., & Chen, R. (1994). Imitation and expression of facial affect in autism. *Development and Psychopathology, 6,* 433–444.

Mahler, M. (1952). On child psychosis and schizophrenia: Autistic and symbiotic infantile psychoses. *Psychoanalytic Study of the Child, 7,* 286–305.

Maurice, C. (1993). *Let me hear your voice.* New York: Knopf.

McAdoo, W. G., & DeMyer, M. K. (1978). Personality characteristics of parents. In M. Rutter & E. Schopler (Eds.), *Autism: A reappraisal of concepts and treatment* (pp. 251–267). New York: Plenum.

McDougle, C. J., Price, L. H., Volkmar, F. R., Goodman, W. K., Ward-O'Brian, D., Nielsen, J., Bregman, J., & Cohen, D. J. (1992). Clomipramine in autism: Preliminary evidence of efficacy. *Journal of the American Academy of Child and Adolescent Psychiatry, 31,* 746–750.

Meltzoff, A. N., & Gopnik, A. (1993). The role of imitation in understanding persons and developing a theory of mind. In S. Baron-Cohen, H. Tager-Flusberg, & D. J. Cohen (Eds.), *Understanding other minds: Perspectives from autism* (pp. 335–366). Oxford, England: Oxford University Press.

Mesibov, G. B. (1986). A cognitive program for teaching social behaviors to verbal autistic adolescents and adults. In E. Schopler & G. B. Mesibov (Eds.), *Social behavior in autism* (pp. 265–303). New York: Plenum.

Mesibov, G. B. (1996). Division TEACCH: A program model for working with autistic people and their families. In M. C. Roberts (Ed.), *Model practices in service delivery in child and family mental health* (pp. 215–230). Hillsdale, NJ: Erlbaum.

Mesibov, G. B., Schopler, E., & Hearsey, K. A. (1994). Structured teaching. In E. Schopler & G. B. Mesibov (Eds.), *Behavioral issues in autism* (pp. 195–207). New York: Plenum.

Mesibov, G., Schopler, E., Schaffer, B., & Landrus, R. (1988). *Individualized assessment and treatment for autistic and developmentally disabled children: Vol. 4. Adolescent and Adult Psychoeducational Profile (AAPEP).* Austin, TX: Pro-Ed.

Mesibov, G. B., & Shea, V. (1996). Full inclusion and students with autism. *Journal of Autism and Developmental Disorders, 26,* 337–346.

Minshew, N. (1996). Brief report: Brain mechanisms in autism: Functional and structural abnormalities. *Journal of Autism and Developmental Disorders, 26,* 205–209.

Minshew, N. J., & Goldstein, G. (1993). Is autism an amnesic disorder?: Evidence from the California Verbal Learning Test. *Neuropsychology, 7,* 1–8.

Mundy, P., & Sigman, M. (1989). The theoretical implications of joint-attention deficits in autism. *Development and Psychopathology, 1,* 173–183.

Mundy, P., Sigman, M., Ungerer, J., & Sherman, T. (1986). Defining the social deficits of autism: The contribution of nonverbal communication measures. *Journal of Child Psychology and Psychiatry, 27,* 657–669.

National Institutes of Health. (1990). Consensus development conference statement: Treatment of destructive behaviors in persons with developmental disabilities. *Journal of Autism and Developmental Disorders, 20,* 403–429.

Ornitz, E. M. (1971). Childhood autism: A disorder of sensorimotor integration. In M. Rutter (Ed.), *Infantile autism: Concepts, characteristics, and treatment* (pp. 50–68). London: Churchill Livingstone.

Ornitz, E. M. (1978). Neurophysiologic studies. In M. Rutter & E. Schopler (Eds.), *Autism: A reappraisal of concepts and treatment* (pp. 117–139). New York: Plenum.

Ornitz, E. M. (1989). Autism. In C. G. Last & M. Hersen (Eds.), *Handbook of child psychiatric diagnosis.* (pp. 233–278). New York: Wiley.

Ornitz, E. M., Forsythe, A. B., & de la Peña, A. (1973). Effect of vestibular and auditory stimulation on the REMs of REM sleep in autistic children. *Archives of General Psychiatry, 29,* 786–791.

Osterling, J., & Dawson, G. (1994). Early recognition of children with autism: A study of first birthday home videotapes. *Journal of Autism and Developmental Disorders, 24,* 247–257.

Ozonoff, S. (1995). Executive function impairments in autism. In E. Schopler & G. Mesibov (Eds.), *Learning and cognition in autism* (pp. 199–220). New York: Plenum.

Ozonoff, S., & McEvoy, R. (1994). A longitudinal study of executive function and theory of mind development in autism. *Development and Psychopathology, 6,* 415–431.

Ozonoff, S., Pennington, B. F., & Rogers, S. J. (1991). Executive function deficits in high-functioning autistic individuals: Relationship to theory of mind. *Journal of Child Psychology and Psychiatry and Allied Disciplines, 32,* 1081–1105.

Ozonoff, S., Rogers, S., & Pennington, B. F. (1991). Asperger's syndrome: Evidence of an empirical distinction from high-functioning autism. *Journal of Child Psychology and Psychiatry, 32,* 1107–1122.

Pacquier, P. F., Van Dongen, H. R., & Loonen, C. B. (1992). The Landau–Kleffner syndrome or "acquired aphasia with convulsive disorder": Long-term follow-up of six children and a review of recent literature. *Archives of Neurology, 49,* 354–359.

Panksepp, J. (1979). A neurochemical theory of autism. *Trends in Neuroscience, 2,* 174–177.

Payton, J. B., Steele, M. W., Wegner, S. L., & Minshew, N. J. (1989). The fragile X marker and autism in perspective. *Journal of the American Academy of Child and Adolescent Psychiatry, 28,* 417–421.

Phelps, L., & Grabowski, J. (1991). Autism: Etiology, differential diagnosis, and behavioral assessment update. *Journal of Psychopathology and Behavioral Assessment, 13,* 107–125.

Piven, J., Arndt, S., Bailey, J., Havercamp, S., Andreasen, N., & Palmer, P. (1995). An MRI study of brain size in autism. *American Journal of Psychiatry, 152,* 1145–1149.

Piven, J., Berthier, M. L., Starkstein, S. E., Nehme, E., Pearlson, G., & Folstein, S. (1990). Magnetic resonance imaging evidence for a defect of cerebral cortical development in autism. *American Journal of Psychiatry, 147,* 734–739.

Piven, J., Tsai, G., Nehme, E., Coyle, J. T., Chase, G. A., & Folstein, S. (1991). Platelet serotonin, a possible marker for familial autism. *Journal of Autism and Developmental Disorders, 21,* 51–59.

Pollack, M., & Krieger, H. P. (1958). Oculomotor and postural patterns in schizophrenic children. *Archives of Neurology and Psychiatry, 79,* 720–726.

Prior, M., & Chen, C. (1976). Short-term and serial memory in autistic, retarded, and normal children. *Journal of Autism and Childhood Schizophrenia, 6,* 121–131.

Prior, M., & Hoffman, W. (1990). Neuropsychological testing of autistic children through an exploration with frontal lobe tasks. *Journal of Autism and Developmental Disorders, 20,* 581–590.

Rank, B. (1949). Adaptation of the psychoanalytic technique for the treatment of young children with atypical development. *American Journal of Orthopsychiatry, 19,* 130–139.

Reiss, A. L., & Freund,. L. (1990). Fragile X syndrome, DSM-III-R, and autism. *Journal of the American Academy of Child and Adolescent Psychiatry, 29*, 885–891.

Riguet, C., Taylor, N., Benaroya, S., & Klein, L. (1981). Symbolic play in autistic, Down's, and normal children of equivalent mental age. *Journal of Autism and Developmental Disorders, 11*, 439–448.

Rimland, B. (1964). *Infantile autism*. Englewood Cliffs, NJ: Prentice-Hall.

Rimland, B. (1992a). Facilitated communication: What's going on? *Autism Research Review International, 6*, 2–3.

Rimland, B. (1992b, May). *Autism: A historical perspective*. Paper presented at the 13th Annual TEACCH Conference, Chapel Hill, NC.

Ritvo, E. R., & Freeman, B. J. (1977). National Society for Autistic Children definition of the syndrome of autism. *Journal of Pediatric Psychology. 2*, 146–148.

Ritvo, E. R., Freeman, B. J., Pingree, C., Mason-Brothers, A., Jorde, L., Jenson, W. R., McMahon, W. M., Petersen, P. B., Mo, A., & Ritvo, A. (1989). The UCLA–University of Utah epidemiologic survey of autism: Prevalence. *American Journal of Psychiatry, 146*, 194–199.

Ritvo, E. R., Freeman, B. J., Scheibel, A. B., Duong, T., Robinson, H., Guthrie, D., & Ritvo, A. (1986). Lower purkinje cell counts in the cerebella of four autistic subjects: Initial findings of the UCLA–NSAC autopsy research report. *American Journal of Psychiatry, 143*, 862–866.

Ritvo, E. R., Jorde, L. B., Mason-Brothers, A., Freeman, B. J., Pingree, C., Jones, M. B., McMahon, W. M., Petersen, P. B., Jenson, W. R., & Mo, A. (1989). The UCLA–University of Utah epidemiologic survey of autism: Recurrence risk estimates and genetic counseling. *American Journal of Psychiatry, 146*, 1032–1036.

Ritvo, E. R., Ornitz, E. M., Eviatar, A., Markham, C. H., Brown, M. B., & Mason, A. (1969). Decreased postrotatory nystagmus in early infantile autism. *Neurology, 19*, 653–658.

Ritvo, E. R., Rabin, K, Yuwiler, A., Freeman, B. J., & Geller, E. (1978). Biochemical and hematologic studies: A critical review. In M. Rutter & E. Schopler (Eds.), *Autism: A reappraisal of concepts and treatment* (pp. 163–183). New York: Plenum.

Ritvo, E. R., Yuwiler, A., Geller, E., Ornitz, E. M., Saeger, K., & Plotkin, S. (1970). Increased blood serotonin and platelets in early infantile autism. *Archives of General Psychiatry, 23*, 566–572.

Rumsey, J. M., & Hamburger, S. D. (1988). Neuropsychological findings in high-functioning men with infantile autism, residual state. *Journal of Clinical and Experimental Neuropsychology. 10*, 201–221.

Rumsey, J. M., Rapoport, J. L., & Sceery, W. R. (1985). Autistic children as adults: Psychiatric, social, and behavioral outcomes. *Journal of the American Academy of Child Psychiatry, 24*, 465–473.

Ruttenberg, B. A. (1971). A psychoanalytic understanding of infantile autism and its treatment. In D. W. Churchill, G. D. Alpern, & M. K. DeMyer (Eds.), *Infantile autism: Proceedings of the Indiana University Colloquium* (pp. 145–184). Springfield, IL: Charles C. Thomas.

Rutter, M. (1967). Psychotic disorders in early childhood. In A. Coppen & A. Walk (Eds.), *Recent developments in schizophrenia: A symposium* (pp. 133–158). Kent, England: Headley Brothers Ltd.

Rutter, M. (1968). Concepts of autism: A review of research. *Journal of Child Psychology and Psychiatry, 9*, 1–25.

Rutter, M. (1978a). Diagnosis and definition. In M. Rutter & E. Schopler (Eds.), *Autism: A reappraisal of concepts and treatment* (pp. 1–25). New York: Plenum.

Rutter, M. (1978b). Etiology and treatment: Cause and cure. In M. Rutter & E. Schopler (Eds.), *Autism: A reappraisal of concepts and treatment* (pp. 327–335). New York: Plenum.

Rutter, M. (1978c). Language Disorder and Infantile Autism. In M. Rutter & E. Schopler (Eds.), *Autism: A reappraisal of concepts and treatment* (pp. 85–104). New York: Plenum.

Rutter, M. (1983). Cognitive deficits in the pathogenesis of autism. *Journal of Child Psychology and Psychiatry, 24,* 513–531.

Rutter, M., & Bartak, L. (1971). Causes of infantile autism: Some considerations from recent research. *Journal of Autism and Childhood Schizophrenia, 1,* 20–32.

Rutter, M., Bartak, L., & Newman, S. (1971). Autism: A central disorder of cognition and language? In M. Rutter (Ed.), *Infantile autism: Concepts, characteristics, and treatment* (pp. 148–171). London: Churchill Livingstone.

Rutter, M., Greenfeld, D., & Lockyer, L. (1967). A five to fifteen year follow-up study of infantile psychosis. II. Social and behavioural outcome. *British Journal of Psychiatry, 113,* 1183–1199.

Rutter, M., & Lockyer, L. (1967). A five to fifteen year follow-up study of infantile psychosis: I. Description of sample. *British Journal of Psychiatry, 113,* 1169–1182.

Rutter, M., Macdonald, H., Le Couteur, A., Harrington, R., Bolton, P., & Bailey, A. (1990). Genetic factors in child psychiatric disorders: II. Empirical findings. *Journal of Child Psychology and Psychiatry, 31,* 39–83.

Saitoh, O., Courchesne, E., Egaas, B., Lincoln, A. J., & Schreibman, L. (1995). Cross-sectional area of the posterior hippocampus in autistic patients with cerebellar and corpus callosum abnormalities. *Neurology, 45,* 317–324.

Sandman, C. A., Barron, J. L., Chicz-DeMet, A., & DeMet, E. M. (1991). Brief report: Plasma B-endorphin and cortisol levels in autistic patients. *Journal of Autism and Developmental Disorders, 21,* 83–87.

Schain, R. J., & Yannet, H. (1960). Infantile autism: An analysis of 50 cases and a consideration of certain neurophysiologic concepts. *Journal of Pediatrics, 57,* 560–567.

Schopler, E., Andrews, C. E., & Strupp, K. (1979). Do autistic children come from upper-middle-class parents? *Journal of Autism and Developmental Disorders, 9,* 139–152.

Schopler, E., & Mesibov, G. B. (Eds.). (1994). *Behavioral issues in autism.* New York: Plenum.

Schopler, E., Reichler, R., Bashford, A., Lansing, M., & Marcus, L. (1990). *Individualized assessment and treatment for autistic and developmentally disabled children: Vol. 1. Psychoeducational Profile-Revised (PEP-R).* Austin, TX: Pro-Ed.

Schopler, E., Reichler, R., & Renner, B. (1988). *The Childhood Autism Rating Scale (CARS).* Los Angeles, CA: Western Psychological.

Schopler, E., Short, A., & Mesibov, G. B. (1989). Relation of behavioral treatment to "normal functioning": Comment on Lovaas. *Journal of Consulting and Clinical Psychology, 57,* 1–3.

Schopler, E., Van Bourgondien, M., & Bristol, M. (Eds.). (1993). *Preschool issues in autism.* New York: Plenum.

Schreibman, L., Loos, L. M., & Stahmer, A. C. (1993). Autistic disorder. In R. T. Ammerman, C. G. Last, & M. Hersen (Eds.), *Handbook of prescriptive treatments for children and adolescents* (pp. 9–27). MA: Allyn & Bacon.

Schuler, A., & Prizant, B. (1985). Echolalia. In E. Schopler & G. Mesibov (Eds.), *Communication problems in autism* (pp. 163–184). New York: Plenum.

Shah, A., & Frith, U. (1993). Why do autistic individuals show superior performance on the Block Desiogn test? *Journal of Child Psychology and Psychiatry, 34,* 1351–1364.

Shane, H. C. (1994). *Facilitated communication: The clinical and social phenomenon.* San Diego, CA: Singular.

Shea, V., & Mesibov, G. B. (1985). Brief report: The relationship of learning disabilities and higher-level autism. *Journal of Autism and Developmental Disorders, 15,* 425–435.

Siegel, B., Vukicevic, J., & Spitzer, R. L. (1990). Using signal detection methodology to revise DSM-III-R: Re-analysis of the DSM-III-R national field trials for Autistic Disorder. *Journal of Psychiatric Research, 24,* 293–311.

Skinner, B. F. (1953). *Science and human behavior.* New York: Macmillan.

Smalley, S. L., Asarnow, R. F., & Spence, A. (1988). Autism and genetics: A decade of research. *Archives of General Psychiatry, 45,* 953–961.

Smalley, S. L., Tanguay, P. E., Smith, M., & Gutierrez, G. (1992). Autism and tuberous sclerosis. *Journal of Autism and Developmental Disorders, 22,* 339–355.

Stefanatos, G. A., Grover, W., & Geller, E. (1995). Case study: Corticosteroid treatment of language regression in pervasive developmental disorders. *Journal of the American Academy of Child and Adolescent Psychiatry, 34,* 1107–1111.

Steffenburg, S., Gillberg, C., Hellgren, L., Andersson, L., Gillberg, I. C., Jakobsson, G., & Bohman, M. (1989). A twin study of autism in Denmark, Finland, Iceland, Norway, and Sweden. *Journal of Child Psychology and Psychiatry, 30,* 405–416.

Stone, W. L., & Hogan, K. L. (1993). A structured parent interview for identifying young children with autism. *Journal of Autism and Developmental Disorders, 23,* 639–652.

Strain, P. (1984). Social interactions of handicapped preschoolers in developmentally integrated and segregated settings: A study of generalization effects. In T. Field, J. Roopharine, & M. Segal (Eds.), *Friendships in normal and handicapped children* (pp. 187–207). Norwood, NJ: Ablex Publishing Corporation.

Sturgis, E. T. (1993). Obsessive–Compulsive Disorders. In P. B. Sutker & H. E. Adams (Eds.), *Comprehensive handbook of psychopathology* (pp. 129–144). New York: Plenum.

Swedo, S. E., & Rapoport, J. L. (1990). Obsessive Compulsive Disorder in Childhood. In M. Hersen & C. G. Last (Eds.), *Handbook of child and adult psychopathology: A longitudinal perspective* (pp. 211–219). New York: Pergamon.

Szatmari, P. (1991). Asperger's syndrome: Diagnosis, treatment, and outcome. *Psychiatric Clinics of North America, 14,* 81–93.

Szatmari, P., Bremner, R., & Nagy, J. (1989). Asperger's syndrome: A review of clinical features. *Canadian Journal of Psychiatry, 34,* 554–560.

Szatmari, P., Jones, M. B., Tuff, L., Bartolucci, G., Fisman, S., & Mahoney, W. (1993). Lack of cognitive impairment in first-degree relatives of children with pervasive developmental disorders. *Journal of the American Academy of Child and Adolescent Psychiatry, 32,* 1264–1273.

Taft, L. T., & Goldfarb, W. (1964). Prenatal and perinatal factors in childhood schizophrenia. *Developmental Medicine and Child Neurology, 6,* 32–43.

Tager-Flusberg, H. (1989). A psycholinguistic perspective on language development in the autistic child. In G. Dawson (Ed.), *Autism: Nature, diagnosis, and treatment* (pp. 92–115). New York: Guilford.

Tager-Flusberg, H. (1991). Semantic processing in the free recall of autistic children: Further evidence for a cognitive deficit. *British Journal of Developmental Psychology, 9,* 417–430.

Tager-Flusberg, H. (1993). What language reveals about the understanding of minds in children with autism. In S. Baron-Cohen, H. Tager-Flusberg, & D. J. Cohen (Eds.), *Understanding other minds: Perspectives from autism* (pp. 138–157). Oxford, England: Oxford University Press.

Tsai, L. (1987). Pre-, peri-, and neonatal factors in autism. In E. Schopler & G. Mesibov (Eds.), *Neurobiological issues in autism* (pp. 179–189). New York: Plenum.

Tsai, L. Y., Stewart, M. A., Faust, M., & Shook, S. (1982). Social class distribution of fathers of children enrolled in the Iowa Autism Program. *Journal of Autism and Developmental Disorders, 12,* 211–221.

Ungerer, J., & Sigman, M. (1987). Categorization skills and receptive language development in autistic children. *Journal of Autism and Developmental Disorders, 17,* 3–16.

Volkmar, F. R. (1991). Autism and the Pervasive Developmental Disorders. In M. Lewis (Ed.), *Child and adolescent psychiatry: A comprehensive textbook.* (pp. 499–508). Baltimore: Williams & Wilkins.

Volkmar, F. R., Cicchetti, D. V., Bregman, J., & Cohen, D. J. (1988). Three diagnostic systems for autism: DSM-III, DSM-III-R, and ICD-10. *Journal of Autism and Developmental Disorders, 22,* 483–492.

Volkmar, F. R., & Cohen, D. J. (1991). Debate and argument: The utility of the term Pervasive Developmental Disorder. *Journal of Child Psychology and Psychiatry, 32,* 1171–1172.

Volkmar, F. R., Klin, A., Siegel, B., Szatmari, P., Lord, C., Campbell, M., Freeman, B. J., Cicchetti, D. V., Rutter, M., Kline, W., Buitelaar, J., Hattab, Y., Fombonne, E., Fuentes, J., Werry, J., Stone, W., Kerbeshian, J., Hoshino, Y., Bregman, J., Loveland, K., Szymanski, L., & Towbin, K. (1994). Field trial for Autistic Disorder in DSM-IV. *American Journal of Psychiatry, 151,* 1361–1367.

Volkmar, F. R., & Nelson, D. S. (1990). Seizure disorders in autism. *Journal of the American Academy of Child and Adolescent Psychiatry, 29,* 127–129.

Volkmar, F. R., Paul, R., & Cohen, D. (1985). The use of "Asperger's syndrome." *Journal of Autism and Developmental Disorders, 15,* 437–439.

Walker, H. A. (1977a). A dermatoglyphic study of autistic patients. *Journal of Autism and Childhood Schizophrenia, 7,* 11–21.

Walker, H. A. (1977b). Incidence of minor physical anomaly in autism. *Journal of Autism and Childhood Schizophrenia, 7,* 165–176.

Wing, L. (1980). Childhood autism and social class: A question of selection? *British Journal of Psychiatry, 137,* 410–417.

Wing, L. (1981). Asperger's syndrome: A clinical account. *Psychological Medicine, 11,* 115–129.

Wing, L., & Gould, J. (1979). Severe impairments of social interaction and associated abnormalities in children: Epidemiology and classification. *Journal of Autism and Developmental Disorders, 9,* 11–29.

Wolfensberger, W. (1972). *The principle of normalization in human services.* Toronto: National Institute on Mental Retardation.

World Health Organization. (1978). *International classification of diseases* (9th ed.). Geneva: Author.

World Health Organization. (1992). *International classification of diseases* (10th ed.). Geneva: Author.

Index

A "*t*" suffix to a page number indicates that a term is mentioned in a table.

AAPEP: *see* Adolescent and Adult Psychoeducational Profile
Activities, in autism diagnosis, 24
ADD: *see* Attention deficit disorder
ADI-R: *see* Autism Diagnostic Interview-Revised
Adolescent and Adult Psychoeducational Profile, 85, 89
ADOS: *see* Autism Diagnostic Observation Scale
Agriculture, living environments based on, 97–98
Aloneness, 5
American Psychiatric Association, 28–30
Amnesia, 69–70
Amphetamines, 80
Amygdala, abnormal findings, 53–54
Anoxia, intrauterine, 11
   Rimland on, 11–12
Anticonvulsants, 79
Antidepressants, 80
APA: *see* American Psychiatric Association
Asperger's disorder, 30, 31
   in autism differential diagnosis, 35, 36–37
Assessment tools, structured teaching, 85–89
Attention, 71–73
   selective, 72
   sharing experiences and, 73
   stimulus overselectivity and, 71–72
   sustained, 72–73
Attention deficit disorder
   in autism differential diagnosis, 39–40
   treatment of, 80
Autism
   defining: *see* Definitions, of autism
   diagnosis: *see* Diagnosis
   epidemiology: *see* Epidemiological data

Autism Diagnostic Interview-Revised, 28
Autism Diagnostic Observation Scale, 27
Autism spectrum disorder, 31–32
Aversive procedures, controversy over, 101–102

Behavior
   in autism diagnosis, 24
   modification of: *see* Educational/behavioral interventions
Behavioral formulations, early, 15–17
Behavioral interventions: *see* Educational/behavioral interventions
Beta-blockers, 81
Biological interventions: *see* Medical interventions
Biological theories
   Bettelheim on, 7–8
   current, 45–63
      cortical electroencephalographic findings, 56–60
      genetic findings, 45–50
      neuroanatomical findings, 51–56
      neurochemical findings, 60–62
      prenatal and perinatal complications, 50–51
   history of, 10–13
      congenital rubella, 12
      EEG studies, 10
      hyperoxia, 11–12
      nystagmus, 11
      physical anomalies, 12–13
      prenatal and perinatal insults, 11
      seizures, 10
Birth order, 51

Birth trauma, 11
Bittersweet Farms, 98
Blindness, 17
Brain activity: *see* Electroencephalographic
    studies
Brain opioids, 61–62
Brain size, 55
"Building a person" theory, 17

Carolina Living and Learning Center, 98
CARS: *see* Childhood Autism Rating Scale
Categorization, 70–71
CDD: *see* Childhood disintegrative disorder
Cerebellum, abnormal findings, 52–53
Cerebral cortex, abnormal findings, 54–55
Childhood Autism Rating Scale, 26
Childhood disintegrative disorder, 30, 31, 35
    in autism differential diagnosis, 36
Childhood onset developmental disorder, 31
CLLC: *see* Carolina Living and learning Center
Clomipramine, 80
"Closed-loop phenomena," 15
Cognition
    abnormalities, 46–47
    attention and, 71–73
    executive functions and, 74–75
    memory and, 69–71
    theory of mind and, 73–74
Cognitive behavioral approaches, to interven-
        tion, 84–85, 86t, 87t–88t, 89t
Communication, *see also* Language abilities
    facilitated, controversy over, 103–104
    verbal and nonverbal, in autism diagnosis,
        22–23
Concentration camp victims, 8
Conceptualization, 15
Congenital rubella, 12
Conversation, language abilities and, 67–68
COPDD: *see* Childhood onset developmental
    disorder

Definitions, of autism
    history of, 28–31
    Kanner's, 5–6
    as pervasive development disorder: *see* Per-
        vasive developmental disorder
Deprivation
    emotional, Bettelheim on, 7–8
    sensory, 12

Developmental language disorders, in autism
    differential diagnosis, 41–42
Developmental receptive aphasia, 41–42
Dexedrine, 80
Diagnosis
    associated characteristics and, 25–26
    current criteria for, 21–24
        and Kanner's criteria compared, 21t
        reciprocal social interaction, 21–22
        restricted repertoire of activities and inter-
            ests, 24
        verbal and nonverbal communication, 22–24
    differential diagnosis, 35–43, 43t
    early markers for, 25
    labels, 20
    signal detection studies and, 24–25
    tools for, 26–28
Diagnostic and Statistical Manual
    DSM-III, 28–29
    DSM-III-R, 29–30
    DSM-IV, 30
Differential diagnosis, 35–43, 43t
    attention deficit disorder, 39–40
    developmental language disorders, 41–42
    learning disabilities, 38–39, 43t
    mental retardation, 37–38, 43t
    obsessive–compulsive disorder, 40–41
    pervasive developmental disorders, 35–37
    schizophrenia, 42–43, 43t
Division TEACCH
    early intervention programs, 96
    structured teaching, educational goals of, 85–89
DRA: *see* Developmental receptive aphasia
DSM: see Diagnostic and Statistical Manual

Early interventions
    common elements, 95t
    controversy over, 94–97
Echolalia, 5, 15, 66–67
Education, full inclusion in, 98–99
Educational/behavioral interventions, 82–91
    cognitive behavioral approaches, 84–85, 86t,
        87t–88t, 89t
    Ferster's contributions to, 16
    Lovaas' contributions to, 16–17
    operant approaches, 82–84
    social learning approaches, 86, 88–90
EEG: *see* Electroencephalographic studies
Ego-dystonia, 41

Electroencephalographic studies, 56–60
    activity patterns, 56
        across brain regions, 56–57
    early studies, 10
    hemispheric lateralization, 56–57
    Landau–Kleffner syndrome, 59
    seizure disorders, 58–59
Emotional deprivation, Bettelheim on, 7–8
Emotional perception, and expression, 68
Employment, controversy over, 99–101
Enclaves (employment), 100
Endorphins, 61–62
Environmental factors
    birth order, 51
    parenting patterns, 6, 7
    psychoanalytical theory and, 9
Environments, agriculture-based, 97–98
Epidemiological data, 32–35
    mental retardation, 34
    prevalence, 32–34
    sex ratios, 33–34
    social class distribution, 34–35
Equilibrium, disturbances of, 11
Executive functions, 74–75
Expression, emotional perception and, 68

Facilitated communication, controversy over,
        103–104
Family studies, 46, 47
FC: see Facilitated communication
Fenfluramine, 81
Fibroplasia, retrolental, 12
Fingerprint studies, 13
Fragile X syndrome, 48–49
Full inclusion, in regular education, 98–99

Genetic theories
    fragile X syndrome and, 48–49
    history of, 13–14
    phenylketonuria and, 49
    social and cognitive impairments and, 46–47
    trisomy of chromosome 15 and, 50
    tuberous sclerosis and, 49–50
    twin and family studies, 45–46

Haldol, 79–80
Head, physical anomalies associated with, 13
Heller's syndrome: see Childhood disintegra-
        tive disorder

Hemispheric lateralization, 14–15
    EEG studies, 56–57
Hippocampus, abnormal findings, 53–54
Hyperoxia, 11–12

Imitation, 24, 74
Impairment
    language, 5–6, 9
    qualitative versus quantitative, 30
    social and cognitive, genetic theories and,
        46–47
Inclusion, in regular education, 98–99
Inderal, 81
Infantile autism
    early manifestations, 3–4
    Kanner's description, 4–5
Infections, viral: see Viral illnesses
Information organization, memory and, 70
Integration, in regular education, 98
Intelligence, 6
Intelligence quotient scores, in twin studies,
        46–47
Interests, in autism diagnosis, 24
Interventions
    biological, 78–82
    early, 94–97
    educational/behavioral, 82–91
    inclusion and, 98–99
    normalization principle and, 97–98
    psychodynamic, 77–78
Interview techniques, psychodynamic interven-
        tion, 78
IQ scores, in twin studies, 46–47
Irrelevant detail, language abilities and, 67
Isolation, social: see Social isolation

Job coach model, 100
Joint attention skills, 73

Labeling, 20
    controversy over, 102–103
Landau–Kleffner syndrome, EEG studies, 59
Language
    in autism diagnosis, 22–23
    developmental disorders, in autism differen-
        tial diagnosis, 41–42
    impairments, 5–6, 9
    memory and, 71

Language abilities, 65–68
  pragmatic aspects, 67–68
  semantic aspects, 66–67
Lateralization, hemispheric, 14–15
  EEG studies, 56–57
Learning disabilities, in autism differential diagnosis, 38, 43t
Learning theory, and autism, 16–17
LEEP Project (Pittsburgh), 96
Limbic system, abnormal findings, 53–54
Literalness, 5
Lithium, 81
Living environments, agriculture-based, 97–98

Mainstreaming, 98
Maternal age, 51
Medical interventions, 78–82
  anticonvulsants, 79
  beta-blockers, 81
  fenfluramine, 81
  lithium, 81
  megavitamin therapy, 81–82
  naltrexone, 81
  neuroleptics, 79–80
  stimulants, 80
  tricyclic antidepressants, 80
Megavitamin therapy, 81–82
Mellaril, 80
Memory, 69–71; see also Rote memory skills
  amnesia and, 68–69
  categorization and, 70–71
  and complex information, 70
  short-term, 70
  words, 40
Mental retardation, 12, 34
  in autism differential diagnosis, 37–38, 43t
Mind, theory of, 73–74
Minnesota Multiphasic Personality Inventory (MMPI), 9
Mobile crews, 100
Mothering, 7, 8
  Ruttenberg on, 7

Naltrexone, 81
National Society for Autistic Children, 28
Neuroanatomical findings, 51–56
  brain size, 55
  cerebellum, 52–53

Neuroanatomical findings (cont.)
  cerebral cortex, 54–55
  limbic system, 53–54
Neurobiological theories: see Biological theories
Neurochemical theories, 14, 60–62
  brain opioids studies, 61–62
  serotonin studies, 60–61
Neuroleptics, 79–80
Neurological dysfunction, 14–15
  hemispheric lateralization, 14–15, 56–57
  neurochemical theories of: see Neurochemical theories
  reticular formation, 15
Nonverbal communication, in autism diagnosis, 22–23
Normalization principle, controversy over, 97–98
NSAC: see National Society for Autistic Children
Nystagmus, 11

Object relationships, 5, 7
Obsessive–compulsive disorder
  in autism differential diagnosis, 40–41
  treatment of, 80
OCD: see Obsessive–compulsive disorder
Operant training techniques, 82–84
Opioid peptides, 61–62
Overattentiveness, 71, 72
Overoxygenation, 11–12
Oxygen
  deficits: see Anoxia
  excesses, 11–12

Parent Interview for Autism, 27–28
Parenting patterns, 6
  as mediating factor, 7
Parents, personality traits, 9–10
PDD-NOS: see Pervasive development disorder not otherwise specified
PDDs: see Pervasive developmental disorders
Peak skills, 65
PEP-R: see Psychoeducational Profile-Revised
Perinatal complications, 11, 50–51
  physical anomalies and, 13
Perseveration, language abilities and, 67
Personality traits, parental, 9–10
Pervasive development disorder not otherwise specified, in autism differential diagnosis, 35, 36

Pervasive developmental disorders
  autism as, 31–32
  differential diagnosis, 35–37
  syndrome spectrum in, 30
Phenylketonuria, 49
Pheraplay (DesLauriers), 78
Physical anomalies, 12–13
PIA: *see* Parent Interview for Autism
Pimozide, 80
Pittsburgh LEEP Project, early intervention pro-
  grams, 96
PL-ADOS: *see* Prelinguistic Autism Diagnos-
  tic Observation Schedule
Play interview technique, 78
Positive reinforcement, 16
Pragmatism, language abilities and, 67–68
Pregnancy, complications during: *see* Prenatal
  complications
Prelinguistic Autism Diagnostic Observation
  Schedule, 27
Prelinguistic deficits, 73–74
Prenatal complications, 11, 50–51
  physical anomalies and, 13
Preoccupation, in autism diagnosis, 24
Preschool-age children
  early autism manifestations, 3–4
  early intervention in, 94–97
Prevalence, 32
  recent estimates, 32–33
  in siblings, 33
Pronominal reversal, 5, 15, 66
Psychoanalytic theory, 6–8
  arguments against, 8–10; *see also* Biological
    theories
  Kanner's original formulations, 6
  and psychodynamic interventions, 77–78
Psychoeducational Profile-Revised, 85, 87–88
Punishment
  controversy over, 101–102
  and reward, 83–84
  of self-injurious behaviors, 17

Qualitative impairment, 30
Quantitative impairment, 30

Reciprocal social interaction, in autism diagno-
  sis, 21–22
Reinforcement, positive, 16
Residual autism, 29

Responses, 5
Reticular formation, 15
Retrolental fibroplasia, 12
Rett's disorder, 30, 31
  in autism differential diagnosis, 35, 36
Reversal, of pronouns, 5, 15, 66
Reward
  positive reinforcement as, 16
  and punishment techniques, 83–84
Ritalin, 80
Rote memory skills, 15, 65
Rubella, congenital, 12
Rural environments, 97–98

Sameness, 5–6
Schizophrenia, and autism link, 5
  differential diagnosis, 42–43, 43t
School-age child, structured teaching educa-
  tional goals for, 85, 86
Seizures, 10
  EEG studies, 10
Selective attention, 72
Self-destructive behaviors, 16–17
Semantics, language abilities and, 66–67
Sensory deprivation, 12
Serotonin, 60–61
SES: *see* Socioeconomic status
Sex ratios, 33–34
Sheltered workshops, 100–101
Short-term memory, 70
Siblings, prevalence of autism among, 33, 46
Single-mindedness, language abilities and, 67
Small business model, 100
Social abnormalities, 46–47
  limbic system and, 53
  psychoanalytical theory and, 9
Social class, 34–35
Social interaction, reciprocal, in autism diagno-
  sis, 21–22
Social isolation, 5–6
  versus withdrawal, 5
Social learning approaches, 86, 88–90
Social repair strategies, language abilities and,
  67–68
Socioeconomic status, 34–35
Somerset Court (England), 98
Specialization, controversy over, 102–103
Stimulants, 80
Stimulus overselectivity, 71–72

Structured teaching, educational goals, 85–89
Supported employment, controversy over, 99–101
Sustained attention, 72–73

TEACCH
early intervention programs, 96
structured teaching program, 85–89
Tegretal, 79
Tenormin, 81
Theory(ies)
biological/neurobiological formulations,
10–13
early behavioral formulations, 15–17
genetic, 13–14
of mind, cognition and, 73–74
neurochemical, 14
neurological dysfunction, 14–15
psychoanalytic, 6–8
arguments against, 8–10
Thorazine, 80
Treatment: *see* Interventions
Tricyclic antidepressants, 80
Trisomy of chromosome 15, 50

Tuberous sclerosis, 49–50
Twin studies, 45–46
"Two-hit mechanism," 47

Verbal communication, in autism diagnosis,
22–23
Viral illnesses
during pregnancy, 51
rubella, 12
Vitamin B6 therapy, 81–82
Vocational work settings, 99–101

Wechsler Intelligence Scale for Children, in
autism differential diagnosis, 40
"Window of opportunity," early intervention,
96–97
WISC: *see* Wechsler Intelligence Scale for
Children
Withdrawal
from object relationships, 7
in psychoanalytical theory, 9
social isolation versus, 5
Word memorization, 40